images 34

Best of
British Illustration
2010

Association
of illustrators

Images 34

Published by
The Association of Illustrators
2nd Floor, Back Building
150 Curtain Road
London EC2A 3AT
Tel. +44 (0)20 7613 4328
Fax +44 (0)20 7613 4417
info@theaoi.com
theAOI.com
AOImages.com

ISBN 978-0-9558076-7-1

Production in Hong Kong by
Hong Kong Graphics and Printing Ltd
Tel: (852) 2976 0289
Fax: (852) 2976 0292

The Association of Illustrators

Patrons

Contents •

Rod Hunt is a London based Illustrator who has built a reputation for retro tinged Illustrations and detailed character filled landscapes for UK and international clients in publishing, design, advertising and new media, for everything from book covers to advertising campaigns, and even the odd large scale installation. He's also the artist behind the bestselling Top Gear book 'Where's Stig?'

Rod was elected AOI Chairman in September 2009.

Welcome to Images 34, the Best of British Illustration 2010, and my first foreword as the new Chairman of the AOI. I'm immensely proud to be elected to such an important role at the AOI, an organisation that represents the illustration industry in the UK.

Part of the AOI's agenda has always been the continued development of Images as the leading showcase for British Illustration. The competition get tougher every year, so everyone selected for the book should consider themselves a winner, and the award winners truly worthy of accolade.

The past years may have seen a recession in the economy, but not a recession of ideas and talent in British illustration. Young guns, seasoned pros and even a legend or two, Images 34 is as creative, diverse, vibrant and as strong as I've ever seen it.

As the UK's definitive jury selected awards book, commissioners can be confident that Images is the quality resource to enable them to discover the right talent for the job, showcasing the very best of what British illustration has to offer. In these hardened times, picking the very best to deliver that outstanding illustration commission is even more important.

I'm happy to see many new names in the book this year. I remember my own excitement on being selected for Images for the first time (after several unsuccessful attempts I hasten to add), how I felt it validated me as an Illustrator to be seen alongside the people I aspired to be like, and that I'd finally "arrived".

As the stars of tomorrow in the New Talent section take their first steps into their careers, Images gives them one of their first tastes of being a professional illustrator, judged against their peers, by their prospective future employers. I'll expect many of them to be giving us old hands a run for our money in future years.

So enjoy Images 34. I think you will agree that British Illustration is in fine health.

i34 • Foreword

Steven Heller • Co-Chair MFA Designer as Author program, School of Visual Arts, New York.

Steven Heller, author and editor of over 130 books on graphic design, satiric art and popular culture, is the co-founder and co-chair of the MFA Designer as Author program at the School of Visual Arts, New York and also co-founder of the MFA in Design Criticism, MFA in Interaction Design, MFA Social Documentary Film and MPS Branding programs. He has devoted much of his career to fostering design education venues, opportunities and environments.

On the editorial side, for over 40 years he has been an art director for various underground and mainstream periodicals. For 33 years he was an art director at the New York Times (28 of them as senior art director New York Times Book Review). He currently writes the "Visuals" column for the Book Review and "Graphic Content" for the T-Style/The Moment blog. He is editor of AIGA VOICE: Online Journal of Design, a contributing editor to Print, EYE, and Baseline, and a frequent contributor to Metropolis and ID magazines. He contributes regularly to Design Observer and writes the DAILY HELLER blog for Print Magazine (http://blog.printmag. com/dailyheller/). His 130 books include "Design Literacy", "Paul Rand", "Graphic Style" (with Seymour Chwast), "Stylepedia" (with Louise Fili), "The Design Entrepreneur" and "Design School Confidential" (both with Lita Talarico), "Iron Fists: Branding the Twentieth Century Totalitarian State", and most recently "New Ornamental Type" (with Gail Anderson).

He is the recipient of the 1999 AIGA Medal for Lifetime Achievement. His website is hellerbooks.com.

What is crucial to the future of the illustration profession is whether the field's raison d'etre (pardon my French) is relevant in media and image-saturated times. What does illustration contribute today, if anything, that other art forms fail to provide? In other words, what are illustrators saying to the public through their work? And how are they saying it? If they are indeed saying something meaningful (or insightful), are they pushing the various boundaries that need pushing?

After years of studying political, satiric and polemic art dating back to the eighteenth century (remember Daumier, Nast, et al), I have serious doubts that illustration as practiced for the recent past decades – the one-off single image used to illuminate an author's text or sell an advertiser's product – has any real significance in the public arena. Forgive my heresy – I know I must stand up for illustration and illustrators as an integral art form and popular culture – but the trivial ways in which most editorial and advertising illustration is being currently used – as decorative spots and colorful space filler – has marginalized the field and many of the artists in it, who actually do have something to say. Illustrators are shoehorned into small spaces, so much so that a once innocuous word now has dubious implications: The word spot is not just a genre of illustration it is the state of one aspect of the art.

An editorial spot was once an opportunity to test young conceptual abilities – and talent. But today spots are among the most frequent illustration formats. (Yes, I am aware that book and magazine covers are larger than spots, but often the content is no larger than spot size). Even some of the most accomplished illustrators are now forced to do spots because it constitutes the majority of work they are offered. Incidentally doing something small doesn't mean one has more freedom, either. Photographers are routinely afforded big spaces, while illustrators seem to be left with the remains. Spot implies inconsequential, rather than providing meaning. ("Out damn spot!")

Call me old (but I prefer wise), illustration commanded prime editorial real estate during the Sixties throughout the eighties and even into the nineties. Moreover, illustration added visual dimensions beyond the scope of the text. It was often commentary. Which meant it commented on something – a social or political issue.

The verb illustrate meant more than copying a passage from a manuscript and was fairly radical in the Rockwellian era, when the most common illustration métier was a kind of romantic realism, but when "conceptual illustration" finally hit in the sixties, it hit big, like the heavens parted and the lord said commercial art was "the word."

I was introduced to this alternative methodology when, during the late Sixties, Brad Holland, who rebelliously declared to anyone who'd listen he would never merely illustrate but instead would interpret his commissions. Why, he asked, wasn't his visual point of view as valid or profound as a writer's? He fervently believed that illustration should not be subordinate to an author's words and through force of will he convinced editors and art directors of its rightness. He wasn't the only one, but his work on the OpEd page of the New York Times was key in raising the intellectual bar on illustration.

His ideas never mimicked particular passages, but instead served as metaphors representing larger concepts evoked by an author (or himself). If his assignment was, for instance, to illustrate dependence on foreign oil, he adamantly refused to show a predictably contorted Uncle Sam receiving a drug-like "fix" from OPEC (how many times have we seen that uninspired idea?); instead his image was a man pouring a dinosaur from an oil barrel. "Oil" was metaphorically implied, but since the overall image rejected cliché, it forced the viewer to decipher the symbolic code, which in turn triggered a more intense reading of the image.

Big idea-infused "conceptual illustration," which was diametrically opposed to sentimental Rockwellian realism, was adopted as the gold standard of late twentieth century editorial and advertising. While realism has never been entirely expunged, nor should it be, expressionism, surrealism, and even l'art brut emerged as more viable alternatives for the multifaceted editorial content in such concept-based magazines. Abstract and symbolic vocabularies gave illustration more cerebral weight. Illustrations were no longer solely objective mirrors of innocuous content; instead the new breed of "illustrator/journalists" turned their subjective lens towards themes and events that demanded more personal analysis.

The superficial elements of conceptual illustration were, in truth, easily appropriated. Surrealist and expressionist tropes – figurative and landscape dislocations, radical changes in scale, hard-edged woodcut graphics, among others – gave the illusion of intellectual complexity even if the images were void of real content. Consequently conceptual veneers were increasingly common, and style over substance was on the rise throughout the nineties. While this should not imply an entire genre was demeaned, many style-mongers found it easier to make small illustrations that perpetuated the trivial side of illustration. Stock houses have thrived on illustrators who continue to make pictures project a conceptual bent, but are all-purpose templates created with as much feeling as elevator music.

Cultural pundits readily accept that fine art is culturally grander than illustration. Few illustrations are monumental, and most are not meant to endure tests of time. Scale alone does not insure grandeur, and I don't recommend that illustrators compensate by simply making their work larger. But thinking on a larger scale is imperative to raising illustration's bar to new heights. With the advent of graphic novels, Internet animation, artists' toys, and other entrepreneurial wares, illustrators are finding new reasons and outlets for personal expression.

This is not to say that the big thinkers are not making their way through the mass of small thinking. Noma Bar, a brilliant caricaturist routinely stimulates the mind as he tweaks the senses with his visual puns and graphic tricks. Paul Davis makes marks that are both aesthetically pleasing and profound. Illustration is indeed a form of instant messaging and long term stimulating.

So expanding the role of the illustrator into social commentators and critics, as well as inventors and innovators, and ultimately independent thinkers will be the field's best hope.

The marks awarded by the jury for originality,
artistic ability and fulfilment of the brief
determined which images were given an award or
invited to feature in the book.

i34 • Judges
Sarah Coleman • Nol Davis • Penny Garrett

Sarah Coleman • Illustrator and Lettering Artist
A creative all-rounder, Sarah arrived at a full-time career in illustration via extra time served in the bizarre and magical worlds of pirate radio, youth work, the RSC and newspaper obituaries. Creating words and pictures for an international client base for the last sixteen years, she also exhibits in the UK and US. The second and third fingers of her right hand are permanently stained with black ink, which can only be removed (for special occasions) with bleach.

Category • Self Promotion and Design
"I was particularly excited to judge the self-promotional category as this is a subject very close to my heart: the chance to create something off-the-clock and to take a few risks. The high volume of entries made judging difficult, but I was on the lookout for work which, as a fellow illustrator, gave me that nervous excitement you feel when you see something terribly good... and which makes you think 'gosh, must try harder'! The winning entries I chose had that in bucketloads."

Nol Davis • Creative Director, Channel Five
Nol Davis joined Five from Discovery Channel in 1997 to be part of the launch team, and has since overseen every channel look and logo development since. Along the way he has commissioned a mixed bag of musicians and artists; from Lambchop and Faultline to Gerald Scarfe, to contribute to the creativity and presentation of the network. Previously Nol was a history teacher, journalist and abalone shell diver.

Category • New Media, New Talent, Childrens Books
"I was particularly struck by the diverse spectrum of styles, deep conceptualising and fine execution. Having worked mainly in moving images, it's been both inspiring and sobering to see such dynamic and emotive feeling from still media. This quality British illustration should be widely celebrated."

Penny Garrett • Art Director, The Economist newspaper
Penny Garrett manages the graphics department of The Economist newspaper and has done so since 1988. The department is responsible for the design and layout of the print and electronic versions of the magazine, including the front cover. She oversaw the redesign of The Economist, which was launched in full colour for the first time in May 2001. She has also worked for the BBC as Art Director of The Listener magazine and for the Daily Telegraph. Penny obtained a BA (Hons) in Editorial and Information Design at Hornsey College of Art (a very long time ago!)

Category • Editorial, Advertising and Books
"I thought the judging process was organised very efficiently and my fellow judges (mostly) agreed with one another. Overall, there were some excellent submissions to the illustration category, although the advertising section was a little disappointing."

Angus Hyland • Partner, Pentagram Design Ltd.

Angus Hyland is a highly successful designer, writer and curator. He has been a partner at Pentagram London since 1998, and has worked with a wide range of private and public sector clients including, Asprey, BBC, British Council, Citibank, Getty Images, Nokia, Royal Academy, Samsung, Tate Modern and 100% Design.

Angus has won over one hundred creative awards for his work, most notably two D&AD silvers and the Grand Prix at the Scottish Design Awards. He also featured in the Independent on Sunday's 'Top Ten Graphic Designers in the UK' and was elected a member of the Alliance Graphique Internationale (AGI) in 1999.

Since 2005 Angus has been consultant creative director to Laurence King Publishing.

Angus has edited four books on graphic design: 'Pen and Mouse: Commercial Art and Digital Illustration', 'Hand to Eye: Contemporary Illustration', 'C/ID: Visual Identity and Branding for the Arts' (with Emily King) and his bestselling volume on contemporary illustration, 'The Picture Book'.

Category • Self Promotion and Design

Ben Norland • Executive Art Director, Walker Books

Ben graduated from the RCA after studying fine art. As he tried to make a living as a painter, he drifted into the world of children's books and ended up as a full time designer working at Walker Books. He's worked on most every kind of publication for children, from teen fiction to pop-ups and from board books to graphic novels.

Category • Children's Books, New Media and New Talent

"I enjoyed judging a great deal. It was great to see such a broad range of work, much of which was of a very high standard."

Andrew Rae • Illustrator

Andrew Rae is an illustrator and member of the Illustration collective Peepshow (peepshow.org.uk).

He started out producing flyers for club night Perverted Science and has gone on to work for many worldwide clients in advertising, print, publishing and animation including working as Art Director on the BBC 3 show Monkey Dust, directing the on-air identity for MTV Asia and illustrating the identity for The V Festival. His short film the Stunt was screened on Channel 4 in 2007 and his postcard books and prints are available through Concrete Hermit and the Tate Modern shop.

He currently lives and works in London and is represented in the USA by Bernstein and Andriulli. (ba-reps.com/artist/Rae/as/illustrator)

Category • Children's Books, New Media and New Talent

"I was a little apprehensive about judging as I've had bad experiences in the past of fundamental disagreements with other judges that were almost impossible to resolve but this time it was a pleasure and the work spoke for itself."

David Rowley • Freelance Designer and Art Director, London

David Rowley was Design Director of Weidenfeld & Nicolson Illustrated books between 1996 and 2008, and is the creator of a number of best selling and award winning books. These include Michael Palin's Himalaya and books by authors ranging from HRH The Prince of Wales, Helen Mirren, Monty Don and Trinny & Susannah. He also designed the acclaimed and ground-breaking book White Heat by Marco Pierre White. He has worked with illustrators for over twenty-five years.

In 2008 he set up as a freelance designer and art director specialising in illustrated books, and now works for some of the best known publishers in the UK as well as for other clients including Marks & Spencer, for whom he recently designed the 125 year anniversary book, Marks In Time. He is a Fellow of the Chartered Society of Designers, and an Associate member of D&AD. He is also an accomplished photographer.

Category • Books, Editorial and Advertising

"All the award-winning illustrations in the three categories I judged were beautifully crafted, strong on visual narrative and able to resonate emotionally. The overall quality of work in terms of execution and originality of thought made the judging process quite challenging, and clearly the AOI annual exhibition and book remains a highly valuable showcase of contemporary illustration talent."

Matt Small • Client Service Director, Pearlfisher

Matt has always had a big interest in the graphic arts, originally graduating with a degree in Fine Art before going on to complete a post graduate diploma in advertising.

Over ten years in design and branding has seen him hone his design management skills, developing a collaborative approach with clients, designers and illustrators alike to help deliver commercially effective award winning creative work.

Matt is the client service director at Pearlfisher in London.

Category • Self Promotion and Design

"The standard of entries was incredible. I found it a tough but thoroughly enjoyable task – especially when truly engaging pieces of work really stood out and opened my eyes."

Graham Wood • Head of Art, JWT London

Graham Wood joined JWT London in June 2009 as Head of Art, he came from JWT New York where he had been Executive Creative Director, Visual Communications.

Wood, is an award winning designer and creative luminary who spent 15 years as a founding partner of Tomato, London. He works in a variety of media including film, TV, identity design and digital interaction.

At Tomato he worked with brands including Adidas, Porsche, Bacardi, Lexus, Sony Playstation, Orange, Nike, Levi's, MTV, BBC and Reebok.

Wood has also been the recipient of awards including D&AD, AICP, Epica D'Or, Tokyo type, BBC Design Awards and recently directed a promo for Underworld. He has work in the permanent collection at the MOMA New York.

Category • Advertising, Editorial and Books

"A way shall be found before a why shall be found."
Brian Eno

Selected by John Mulholland, Editor, The Observer

John Mulholland took over as Editor of The Observer at the beginning of 2008. In February 2010 he redesigned the paper with a significantly enhanced New Review Section and main section. Prior to that he was Deputy Editor for nine years with specific responsibility for the magazines and weekly features supplements. During that time John was appointed Project Leader overseeing The Observer's transformation from broadsheet to Berliner format. He also spearheaded the development of The Observer's four monthly magazines. Prior to joining The Observer John was Media Editor of The Guardian for four years, consolidating its position as the landmark media section in the UK and later launching it as a stand-alone section.

John has presented a series of media programmes on both radio and TV for the BBC and Channel 4.

John received a BA at Dublin City University, before studying for an MA at California Sate University, Sacramento.

There was a wealth of brilliant work to choose from - over 400 submissions and I enjoyed every one. But I kept coming back to David Hughes. These are striking illustrations and part of their appeal is their mystery: are they playful or melancholic? Are they cheerful or brooding? They don't immediately give themselves up - they require some scrutiny, some time, some patience. The work on Walking the Dog - black and white - can seem dark and even sinister but the dialogue and characters are almost instantly engaging. And wit is deployed liberally in these visualisations. Language too is sprinkled everywhere but it never dominates the illustrations - rather it helps suck you into the characters' world. Hughes work is intricate, sublime, and a little menacing. His portrait of Stravinsky for the New Yorker is inscrutable - no amount of analysis will help you interpret the personality - and for that reason it is all the more compelling. The artistry is delightful but the ambience he creates with his illustrations is every bit as important since it requires attention to detail. By not immediately capturing a person or theme or idea in bold and simple terms, Hughes craft is more subtle and captivating as a result. It rewards prolonged scrutiny and finer dissections. Which is why I kept coming back to the work of David Hughes.

But others I would certainly like to mention: Katherine Baxter, Daniel Pudles, Ian Whadcock, Paul Blow and James Fryer, Paul Cox and Andrew Baker. All of these, for me, had real distinction and caused me hours of trouble as I tried to grapple with a winner. There was so much to admire: from Pudles's bold and imaginative work to Baxter's endearingly original graphic-maps.

And in the New Talent section I was particularly taken by Ollie Stone, Rob Gill, Louise Todd and Chun-Seng Tsou.

Often regarded as the 'enfant terrible' of illustration David Hughes has been an influential presence in the graphic arts for nearly three decades, having begun his working life in TV graphics.

His virtuoso draughtsmanship has graced the pages of numerous magazines and newspapers around the world including The New Yorker, Esquire, The Washington Post, Playboy, The Times and The Guardian.

He has also designed the sets, costumes and props for two operas staged in 1993 and 1998 respectively at the Spoleto Festival in Italy, for which he was awarded the Premio Pegazo Prize for The Rake's Progress.

He has written and published many award winning picture books, including a D&AD Silver Award for Shakespeare's Othello.

In 2003 David Hughes - Drawings was published to accompany a retrospective held at The Wilhelm Busch Museum, Hannover, and in 2006 he creatively defaced, for Walker Books, Victor Hugo's classic The Hunchback of Notre-Dame with 140 uncompromising images, which was the forerunner to his new graphic novel/comic book Walking The Dog published by Jonathan Cape, which is loosely based in a one dimensional, self mocking way on his disenchantment with illustration.

"To have a piece of art created by a dinosaur using the humble pencil in this digital atmosphere selected for the AOI's Critics Award is ironic, inspiring and very satisfying. I drink to John Mulholland and his perfect vision, I thought there must be an age limit, I was wrong."

David Hughes
Walking The Dog

Category Books
Medium Pencil
Brief A page from the graphic novel Walking The Dog. Approaching 50 and warned by his doctor that he's drinking too much and needs to take more exercise the artist is given a dog for his birthday.
Commissioned by Dan Franklin
Client Jonathan Cape
Commissioned for Walking The Dog

Work commissioned for advertising purposes appearing in print and digital media, also television advertising both products and events.

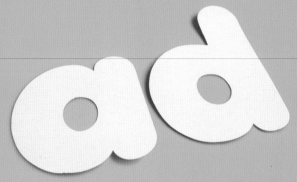

Peter Lyle is a writer and editor from London. He has written on visual culture for newspapers including the Sunday Telegraph, The Guardian and the Independent on Sunday and for magazines including Varoom, Wired and ID. He has developed projects for brands including Motorola, G-Star, Liberty and was editor of Carlos, the award-winning illustrated magazine for Virgin Atlantic. He currently edits the Observer's biannual men's fashion supplement, develops branding projects with influential creative directors Suburbia (the people behind The Face, Pop and Love magazines) and is part of the team behind Manzine, the illustration-heavy, black-and-white side-project that has been one of the most celebrated fanzine launches of recent years.

Last year was, in many respects, a ghastly one for advertising. Brands shrunk their usual budgets for development of visual creative work. Media planners spent less and booked fewer ads, meaning magazines and newspapers either disappeared altogether or felt the squeeze and lost pages and budgets of their own. That in turn meant fewer print advertisements and editorial pages as potential canvases for new illustration. Publishing companies and ad agencies began to doubt the future of print – or even billboards – and look towards a digital future; 2009 was also the year in which "augmented reality" began to be explored as a serious alternative to physical advertising space.

On the other hand, there were still plenty of reasons for champions of illustration to celebrate. The recession may have made the working lives of freelance illustrators harder, but they were less dramatically hit than some visual creatives. High-end photographers and design studios felt the effects of the ad drain immediately – their office overheads and grand concept shoots became unsustainable. Similarly, the people who held the purse strings were forced to look beyond their familiar formulas – and towards underexplored alternatives like illustration – to communicate what they wanted to say about their products and services. And as the post-boom consumer landscape began to take shape, many brands sought to re-establish themselves and their messages by seeking visual values beyond the high-definition gloss that had served so many so well for so long.

There was also more evidence than ever of the contemporary status of illustration as a signifier of luxury and aesthetic taste. James Joyce was asked by Wallpaper* to decorate a Swiss Army Knife for manufacturer Victorinox, while Rob Ryan embellished a Lomo camera for fashion chain Urban Outfitters. Perma-cool American director Spike Jonze made an adult-inflected movie of Maurice Sendak's Where The Wild Things Are. Illustration, sometimes previously pigeonholed as an approach suitable only for selling certain kinds of products to certain kinds of audiences, boasts an enviable cachet

these days. Deployed wisely, it can suggest intimacy, sincerity, painstaking artisanship – ever more precious commodities in an industrialised, increasingly digital world.

Perhaps the most visible illustrated poster of the year was the Stella Artois 4% campaign conceived by London ad agency Mother and realised by veteran American painter and poster artist Robert McGinnis. Like the paintings the beer brand's previous ad agency, Lowe, had previously used, it evoked the art and repro style of vintage advertising imagery, but the 2009 model took the quest for convincingly old-fashioned imagery to another level.

By the end of 2008, when the new lower-alcohol version of the lager brand was announced, Stella Artois with its 5.2 per cent alcohol content, was becoming something of a byword for boozy excess, cited by politicians and frenzied columnists in the last round of theatrical outrage about Britain's prodigious national drinking habit. Rather than sell the new, lower-alcohol Stella 4 % as a diluted, sensible option, Mother chose instead simply to evoke a suaver, sexier era. McGinnis, a veteran of the original posters for films including Breakfast at Tiffany's and Live and Let Die. Though he was in his 70s and ostensibly retired from all but occasional portrait painting, the agency decided to contact McGinnis direct – they had been using his old work as period references for their intended '60s French Riviera feel, and were ultimately seeking "a homage to that era rather than just a parody of it."

This is surely crucial: we've become used to retro kitsch in advertising over the past 15 years, but a true homage aspires to something far more precise and considered – even uncanny. I distinctly remember the first time I saw the first McGinnis Stella 4 % poster looming at me from across the Tube platform. For once, I wasn't wishing my train would arrive – instead, I was scrutinising the poster for flaws or giveaway textures, because it had thrown me a little. Though clearly for a new drink, it looked unmistakably like an authentically old image.

One of the great unseen illustrated posters of the year was also painted entirely by hand. James Goodridge

painted a classic action movie montage poster as a nod to the genre heritage of Quentin Tarantino's World War 2 film Inglourious Basterds. The British-born, L.A.-based illustrator works on movie concept art as well as posters, and though the Goodridge's image wasn't ultimately used as the movie's promotional poster (a more familiar photo comp was instead), it won him warm plaudits (and poster sales) online.

There's plenty to admire if Photoshop masters are able to summon up the tones and patinas of print advertising past with filters and presets, but there's something arresting about McGinnis's Stella Artois posters, in particular, that proves that pre-digital illustration can still refresh the parts no ingenious software solution has yet reached.

There was, of course, plenty of incredibly ingenious digital imagery during the year too. Yuko Shimizu used digital techniques to create a period-inspired campaign for another beer, Tiger, that also evoked the depth and richness of old ink and paper. Alex Trochut's striking way with text and abstract imagery has seen him make shimmering shapes for LG, Nike and Cadbury. A similarly buoyant spirit can be seen in the Coca-Cola posters Mother London commissioned from Los Angeles painter Ronald Kurniawan, gently psychedelic landscapes with nods to '70s graphics and, again, prominent wording from the accompanying TV commercials.

Indeed, textual elements proved to be another recurring theme of the illustrated advertisements of 2009. James Joyce was recruited to create text-and-image posters to pique interest in BBC science show Bang Goes The Theory, while Chris Haughton combined pictures and words to promote the broadcaster's Poetry Season in posters and postcards designed to engage the public. In each case, the words were integral to the image – and the medium chosen to charm the prospective audience in each case was no accident. For Picador, Andy Smith incorporated a quote from a new novel about surfers into a blue-and-white wave image that was used to promote it. A picture might speak a thousand words, but

i34 · Advertising · Essay

Peter Lyle · Writer and Editor

that doesn't mean it can't use a few of them too. Advertisers seem to be cottoning on to the fact that harnessing illustration is about so much more than latching onto a single, vogueish visual style; if they are asked, the right illustrators can do, and sell, pretty much anything you can imagine.

Which just leaves space to add a note about illustration in a post-poster age. Much of the excitement about iPads, other tablets and augmented reality at large – from both brands and publishers – is rooted in the idea that

new technologies will appeal to an advertising industry that is losing faith in and cutting budgets for billboards, posters and ad pages. Gadgets are no longer sold as objects, but as vessels for software, gateways to exciting digital worlds of apps and social networking. Illustrators like Andy Potts are already being called upon to create editorial images that make montages of motifs, silhouettes and symbols that evoke, rather than explain, the magic of new technology – that convey the idea of iPhones, augmented reality and the

rest as new, non-spatial, post-physical ways of navigating the world.

Advertisers haven't quite caught up yet, but it's inevitable that many of them will have by this time next year. In the looming, touch-screen, virtual future, the need to humanise abstract technologies – to make invisible digital data meaningful and emotionally resonant for the average consumer; to differentiate one black, rectangular flat-screened gadget from another, to translate code into human experience – will be more important than ever.

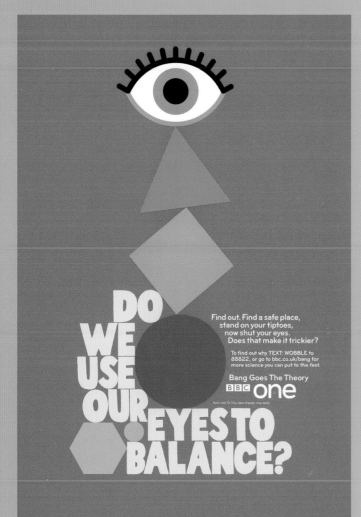

BBC Bang Goes The Theory poster
by James Joyce/Red Bee Media

Stella Artois
by Robert McGinnis/Mother

Coca-Cola poster
by Ronald Kurniawan/Mother

BBC Poetry Season
by Chris Haughton/Premm Design

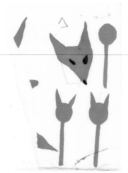

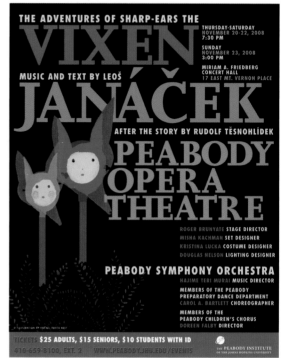

Rachel Tudor Best graduated from Hereford College of Art in 2007 with a BA honours in Illustration. Her approach to illustration is guided by playfulness and instinct. At the beginning of a project she explores a wide range of material, which is often connected with folk tradition and artefacts, animals and her own personal collection of photographs. Rachel thinks her current method of making imagery owes itself to an early childhood obsession with fuzzy felts. She has worked for a range of clients including The Guardian, Granta, Virgin Books and Atlantic Books.

Medium Digital and mixed media
Brief Provide an illustration suitable for use in a poster and programme advertising the opera 'The adventures of sharp ears the vixen'.
Commissioned by Susan Caplan
Client The Peabody Conservatory
Commissioned for Peabody Institute

Medium Ink drawing with digital
Brief One of three billboards created for Tiger Beer advertising in the UK.
Commissioned by Pippa Hall
Client CHI & Partners
Commissioned for Tiger Beer

Yuko Shimizu is originally from Tokyo, Japan, and currently lives and works in New York City.

She has majored in business and worked in corporate PR in Japan for 11 years before she decided to move to New York to study art and pursue her childhood dream. She has received a MFA in Illustration from School of Visual Arts (SVA) and has been working as a freelance illustrator since.

Her clients include: TIME, New York Times, VISA, Pepsi and The Gap. She also teaches at SVA in undergraduate illustration departments and her hobby is to travel around the world for lectures and workshops. She has received Gold and Silver medals from the Society of Illustrators, and is an 8 year regular in the American Illustration annual.

Newsweek Japan has chosen her as one of the "100 Japanese People The World Respects" in 2009.

i34 • Advertising • Bronze

Simon Spilsbury • The Thumbs

Simon Spilsbury is primarily an exponent of line. He draws all the time. His commissioners have described his line as spontaneous, energetic, quirky, inherently humorous, adaptable and elegant. One enthusiastic USA Art Director said "Spilsbury's drawings always jump off the page and bite me on the ass."

Over the past 16 years his work has graced many advertising campaigns, TV programmes/idents and column inches across the globe, including Nike, Virgin, Cobra Beer, The London Election, Martell, Waterstones, Luerzers Archive, The Sunday Times, The Guardian to name a few. He had a two-year column (2007/08) in The Independent with the comedian Dom Joly and regularly writes for The Sunday Times.

His work has won numerous awards, including D&AD Silver, Images 33 Advertising Gold, Campaign Poster Silver, Epica Bronze, Communication Arts, Print Magazine, American Illustration and appeared in Luerzers 200 Best Illustrators.

Medium Ink
Brief Pitch work for the COI's identity card to create characters across the whole demographic via thumbprints.
Commissioned by Simon Pedersen
Client AMV BBDO
Commissioned for Central Office of Information

Work commissioned for adult books, fiction and non-fiction, book jackets and interior illustrations.

David Rowley was Design Director of Weidenfeld & Nicolson Illustrated books between 1996 and 2008, and is the creator of a number of best selling and award winning books. These include Michael Palin's Himalaya and books by authors ranging from HRH The Prince of Wales, Helen Mirren, Monty Don and Trinny & Susannah. He also designed the acclaimed and ground-breaking book White Heat by Marco Pierre White. He has worked with illustrators for over twenty-five years.

In 2008 he set up as a freelance designer and art director specialising in illustrated books, and now works for some of the best known publishers in the UK as well as for other clients including Marks & Spencer, for whom he recently designed the 125 year anniversary book, Marks In Time. He is a Fellow of the Chartered Society of Designers, and an Associate member of D&AD. He is also an accomplished photographer.

On a warm late summer evening last year I switched off my computer and made my way to the frenetic south London streets of the Elephant & Castle. On reaching my destination, a towering monolith of concrete and glass, I walked out of the sunlight and into its cool interior. Here, at the London College of Communication, a fascinating exhibition awaited me.

The AOI has for the last 34 years been hosting this annual exhibition. It is the most revealing and comprehensive showcase of illustration talent chosen from work commissioned over the course of a year. For those selected it is a badge of pride, and for young award winners an important stepping stone to greater recognition. For art directors such as myself, a valuable opportunity to see who is doing what, to discover the new, and to view a rich display of eclectic styles.

Of the several categories in the Images annual, book illustration is the oldest, a centuries-old tradition that is just as commercially relevant to today's publishers as ever before. Books and illustration have always had a close relationship and it is a tradition steeped in beautiful imagery created by many superb and highly influential illustrators such as William Blake, Gustave Doré and E.H. Shephard. This tradition is particularly strong in Britain, where we continue to produce illustrators of exceptional quality by any standards.

The many highly accomplished illustrators whose work appears on the pages of this book can trace their rich European heritage back over 500 years. In the mid-15th century Johann Gutenberg printed the first movable type copies of the 42-line Bible on a wooden printing press, and one cannot overestimate the revolutionary nature of this event. Before Gutenberg, books were hand-illustrated, and a book the size of the Bible would have taken several years to complete in a scriptorium, where monks worked with pen and ink to produce exquisitely rendered text and illuminated initial letters. They were amongst the earliest book illustrators in Europe, and it seems particularly fitting that the most practical means of distributing the work chosen for this years AOI

exhibition is still on a printed page and in the form of a book.

In 1935, the age of the mass market fiction paperback began when Allen Lane launched the extremely successful Penguin imprint. Today, this product is enormously popular in terms of portability and price and represents the most profitable area of British book publishing. The ten original Penguin covers were very simple with flat colour tints and classic Gill Sans type. Within a few years, and increasingly thereafter, illustrators were engaged to convey a sense of genre and content as well as a visual style to help establish author recognition. Their work was on its way to becoming an important marketing tool. Two of the finest British book illustrators of this time were Eric Ravilious and Edward Bawden who created a distinctive visual language both beautiful and poetic.

The work of book illustrators has captivated and delighted adults and children for hundreds of years. When I was a child my mother gave me a copy of The Wind in the Willows illustrated by Arthur Rackham, and enchanted by the warmth and beauty of his work, my lifelong love affair with art and with books began.

David Gentleman was an early favourite, and later Paul Hogarth, Mick Brownfield and Allan Manham, all prolific and widely used at the time. Like all great illustrators they each have (or had) their own style, and there is something unmistakable and inimitable about the quality of their work. Still to this day, I am moved whenever I see David Gentleman's beautiful woodcut illustrations at Charing Cross underground station.

As a book designer and art director I have commissioned illustrators for over twenty-five years and continue to do so as a freelance designer. During my time as Design Director at Weidenfeld & Nicolson, I often chose illustrators to do covers for me, and also commissioned lettering artists to push covers in a fresh and distinctive direction, despite the fact that the nature of the subject matter was nearly always photographic.

I love the character and personality of hand rendered work. There is an immediate appeal and vitality about

something produced by hand. I have drawn since first picking up a crayon, and have always started the design process with pen and paper. Like many designers I have a strong empathy with those who draw and paint for a living. This empathy often overlaps when designers illustrate for themselves, as Saul Bass did to such great effect on the minimal and iconic film posters he designed in the 1950's.

When co-judging for this years annual, I was particularly impressed by James Fryer's work with its powerful combination of idea and draughtsmanship, by Niroot Puttapipat's beautifully crafted mythical silhouettes, and by the vigour and imagination of Simon Pemberton's textural paintings. They each have a very distinctive and recognisable style.

In today's bookshops, people can be overwhelmed by the plethora of books competing for their attention, and a distinctive cover can get a book noticed as well as providing a platform for a strong marketing campaign. It is often the illustrator's individual style that can help provide this distinction, creating something alluring and attention grabbing. Something to covet perhaps. The charm and intrigue of an illustrated cover engages the reader in a way that the ubiquitous vignetted photograph mostly does not. Geoff Grandfield's graphic chalk and pastel illustrations for Raymond Chandler's book of short stories published by The Folio Society in 2008, and Marion Deuchars' beautiful series of George Orwell covers published by Penguin in 2000, are fine examples of this.

This book confirms that illustrators in today's media driven society are in fine voice. Like their forebears they are constantly seeking to engage us with their wit and aesthetic, and in the process thrilling and enchanting people of all ages.

i34 • Books • Essay
David Rowley • Freelance Designer and Art Director

George Orwell Orwell in Spain

George Orwell Orwell and Politics

Frontis, Blackmailers Don't Shoot
by Geoff Grandfield/Folio Society

Orwell book covers
by Marion Deuchars/Penguin

Paradise Lost and Don Quixote
by Gustave Doré

Julius Ceasar book cover
by David Gentleman/Penguin 1976

Midsummer Night's Dream book cover
by David Gentleman/Penguin

The Wind In The Willows
by Arthur Rackham

Simon Pemberton was born near Liverpool and moved to London to study his MA Illustration at Central St Martins. He now lives and works in London's East End with a studio overlooking London Fields. His illustration work has been commissioned by a wide range of major design, publishing and advertising agencies worldwide. Projects are as diverse as brand development, packaging, book covers, editorial and corporate literature.

Clients include Adobe U.K, Fuji, Taylors of Harrogate, The Folio Society, Royal Opera House, Leith Harbour Development, CDT, Lowe, New York Times, L.A Times, Boston Globe, Guardian, Observer, Independent, Blueprint, Financial Times, New Scientist, Tatler, Harper Collins, Penguin, Hodder, Random House Publishing, Readers Digest, BBC Worldwide, etc.

Simon is a previous winner of three Silver awards for Books, Editorial and Design and two Bronze awards in the Design and Advertising sections.

Medium Mixed media
Brief Illustrate the passage "the night was clear and warm... I dragged the bedstead outside the lockup and before dropping off, I travelled around the Southern Cross".
Commissioned by Sheri Gee
Client The Folio Society

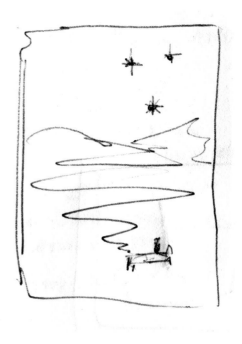

Jonathan Burton grew up in Lincolnshire and has worked as an illustrator since 1999 after graduating with a MA from Kingston University, London. His work has appeared on covers and in the pages of TIME, Nature, New Scientist, The Times and many more magazines and newspapers. Additional clients of note include The Folio Society, The BBC, Saatchi and Saatchi, Mini/BMW and Guinness Book of Records.

He has been the recipient of other awards from the AOI for editorial and advertising illustration as well as from the Society of Illustration in New York. Jonathan now lives with his family in Bordeaux, France.

Medium Pencil and digital
Brief To illustrate a scene from the P.D. James novel 'Cover Her Face' a murder mystery set in 1950's England.
Commissioned by Sheri Gee
Client The Folio Society

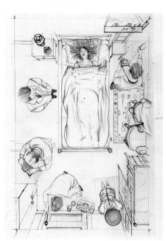

i34 • Books • Bronze
Niroot Puttapipat • The Frog Princess

As a child in his native Chiang Mai, northern Thailand, **Niroot Puttapipat** shared his time between drawing, devouring books, and playing out stories, leading to a lifelong interest in art, literature, history and the natural world. He studied Illustration at Kingston University. Whilst there, his illustrations for the Russian fairytale, The Firebird, were exhibited at Kingston Museum. He is passionately fond of the 'Golden Age' illustrators, Oriental art, and silhouettes. Niroot has illustrated several books for Walker Books and The Folio Society, with subjects ranging from Austen to folk and fairy tales and Omar Khayyam. He now lives in London, and pretends to attribute his questionable health to this fact, though he knows otherwise.

Medium Pen and ink
Brief To read the book and select sixteen scenes to illustrate, supplying full page colour for the Folio Society edition of 'Myths and Legends of Russia'.
Commissioned by Eleanor Crow
Client The Folio Society

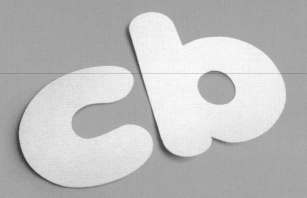

i34 • Children's Books

Work commissioned for children's books, jackets and interior illustrations.

i34 · Children's Books · Essay
Louise Power · Freelance Art Consultant

Louise Power is a freelance Art Consultant primarily working with Walker Books. She is well-known for visiting art colleges around the UK giving talks about illustrating children's books, character development and what publishers look for when artwork and book ideas are submitted. She has had many years experience linking artists with publishers.

In nearly twenty years working for Walker Books – currently as a freelance art consultant – I have been looking at illustration portfolios and illustrators' ideas for children's picture books. I've seen many changes in the portfolios over these years and I'm glad to say they are mostly for the best. However, the market has also changed radically and for illustrators this is not always for the best. Twenty years ago most picture books were written by an author and illustrated by an illustrator. But nowadays there seem to be fewer good texts around, which means that it's harder for an illustrator to find work unless they can also write or at least have ideas for a story. So, an illustrator with good ideas and some ability to write stands a much better chance of being published. I visit many colleges where I give talks and look at portfolios and it seems to me that standards are rising all the time. Nevertheless, there is one fundamental aspect to being a successful illustrator and author of children's books which isn't always thought about enough: the creator of the book doesn't always seem to be quite sure who their audience is.

Who, then, is this audience that picture book creators are trying to captivate and enchant? The answer may be obvious on the surface - the audience for picture books is made up of small children (up to the age of about six in the UK). There are, of course, adults involved too. These are the mums, dads, grannies, aunties, uncles and friends who buy and read the books, the book sellers they buy from, the publishers' sales teams who sell the books to the shops, and the publishers (editors and art directors) who work with the book creator to bring their ideas to life. Despite the importance of these people, it is ultimately the child who is the most crucial member of that audience.

I am the first person to see most of the ideas sent to Walker Books and I can tell which have potential and which do not. Much of the work I see is fantastic, innovative, exciting illustration, but this doesn't always mean it will be appropriate for today's highly competitive and increasingly commercial picture book market. Sadly, many of the beautiful, 'avant-garde' artists' books are almost impossible to publish in the UK. Sometimes this is because the art has a beauty that designers might love but has a sort of coldness which could create a distance from the child. Sometimes it's because the book maker has not yet got the right tone for a children's book. The books that are successful are the ones in which the story has a point and a meaning without being preachy or educative. The pictures in these books have a warmth and emotional quality. To capture both these aspects is not easy, but the books that succeed show an understanding of the audience and of what a picture book is.

Picture Books are for sharing. They are meant to be read aloud, often over and over again as a book becomes a real family favourite. In a successful picture book the words and pictures work together, not in competition but by complementing each other in harmony. Many times the illustrations say much more to the little child, who will 'read' the pictures while listening to the words. The words are, of course, the basic framework for the picture book and it is always the text that publishers consider first. If the words don't work then the book is likely to be rejected however wonderful the art may be. The writer of the story has to say something that is likely to be relevant and of interest to a child's experience. The illustrator takes responsibility for creating the visual world of the story and the characters that inhabit this world. The audience looks at the characters as if they are watching actors in a play. The characters are the most important features of the picture book as they act out the drama, which unfolds through the story. To really engage the audience I believe the illustrator has to show how the characters are feeling. The pictures are, therefore, more than a straightforward set of narrative illustrations; ideally, they should have an underlying emotional content. So although I look for strong observational drawing skills and the ability to create and sustain a character, I am also looking for the potential to depict an emotional world. Through their characters, it is the illustrator's 'job' to express emotions that small children are not able to verbalize or even understand.

At a recent interview with an illustrator who brought in their dummy books to show me, I saw some exquisite illustrations. Yet the characters seemed remote and I realised this was because their faces were not expressive. They were unresponsive to what was happening in the story thereby leaving the audience out in the cold. To feel involved the audience has to see something in the characters' faces and have the chance to get to know them. They also want to see how the characters relate to each other rather than them be shown in isolation or just looking out of the page. In a similar way body language is used to depict feelings, so an acute observation of small children and the way they stand and move is very important. Even when animals are shown in place of children, the illustrator uses their facial and bodily expressions to convey the way the characters deal with what is happening in the story.

This is just a brief personal account of my experience with picture books and my understanding of how the market has changed and how illustrators need to be aware of this so they can adapt. In short, illustrators who can create their own world through their use of words and pictures have an advantage and are more likely to get noticed by publishers. To understand for whom they are writing and illustrating is, in my view, an essential part of creating a successful picture book.

illustration on the left by Chris Haughton

Chris Haughton is an Irish illustrator living in London. He illustrates regularly for The Guardian and The Independent and other publications. He was listed in Time magazine's 'DESIGN 100' in 2007 for the work he has been doing for fair trade clothing company People Tree. His first children's book 'A Bit Lost' will be published in the UK and USA in September 2010 by Walker Books.. His website is at vegetablefriedrice.com

Medium Digital
Brief Interior images for my Children's book about an owl who gets lost. Ages 2-4.
Commissioned by Ines Yoo
Client Borim Press

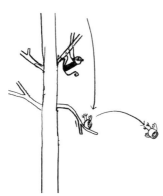

Here she is!
Here is your Mummy!

Medium Digital and mixed media
Brief A spread from one of my stories in development with Templar Publishing.
Commissioned by Mike Jolley
Client Templar Publishing

Jason Chapman studied at Bradford and Camberwell Colleges of Art, and held a variety of jobs to enable him to pursue his illustration career, including balloon seller, road sweeper, and cattery assistant! As well as being Battersea Dogs & Cats Home's 'official illustrator', Jason's illustrations are in permanent exhibitions at the Natural History Museum, Singapore Science Centre and Living Coasts. He works regularly with NSPCC on their successful 'Letters From Santa' campaign.

Jason's characters have been animated (often by himself) for educational DVDs and promotional/web use, which has recently led to development work with Ragdoll Productions.

Becoming a father inspired Jason to develop his own children's books. His debut picture book, 'Ted, Bo and Diz: The First Adventure' was shortlisted for the Best Emerging Illustrator award at the 2007 Booktrust Early Years Awards. 2009 saw seven books published by Simon & Schuster, Campbell Books and Naxos Books. 'Five Little Ducks' was shortlisted at the 2009 Booktrust Early Years Awards. A book with Templar Publishing is due out in 2010.

i34 • Children's Books • Bronze

James de la Rue • Chinese Woman

James de la Rue studied illustration at Bristol UWE and has since illustrated several books for children, including the ongoing 'Gladiator Boy' series by David Grimstone, and Andrew Cope's 'Spy Pups' adventures. In the last three years he has been commissioned by many of the UK's major children's publishers and is represented by Frances McKay.

James was born and grew up on the island of Guernsey and now lives with his wife and two year old daughter near Nottingham. He is often to be found listening to the cricket, when he is not looking forward to listening to the cricket.

Medium Ink
Brief For book eight of Hodder's 'Gladiator Boy' series written by David Grimstone.
Commissioned by Leilani Sparrow
Client Hodder Children's Books

Work commissioned for use in packaging; calendars; merchandising; annual reports; stationery; brochures; catalogues and greeting cards for commercial and private use.

Liz Farrelly is a journalist, editor, curator and broadcaster specialising in design and contemporary culture, and is Editor-at-Large for étapes: international. She has written and edited over 35 books, including For Love and Money: New Illustration and One Hundred at 360: Graphic Design's New Generation, plus three volumes on the art of the business card. Liz teaches Contextual Studies at Central Saint Martins College of Art and Design, London, and the University of Brighton, and lives in Brighton, UK.

I'm a journalist who writes about design, but for most of 2009, I was inundated with illustration and privy to that very different world. Of course, no one makes a living out of writing about design...or illustration for that matter. So, I also make books. I don't say, "I write books"; I do the writing, yes, but there's more to it than that. A team makes a book; the publisher, the editor and my collaborators. And last year we were embroiled in the long, drawn-out process of compiling a very thick book about contemporary illustration, "For Love and Money: New Illustration".

My thoughts? Well, what a different world illustration is to design. It's full of individuals, doing what they love to do best; draw. An interesting bunch. So, I went and got myself more deeply immersed, by co-curating an exhibition about illustration during the "Pick Me Up" fair at Somerset House in Spring 2010. Supplementing these exciting challenges though, is a teaching gig; to a mixed bag of illustrators and graphic designers at the University of Brighton. And that's where I noticed it most, the different mindset between illustrators

and designers. They look different, they dress different, they write very different essays – but they like to collaborate.

Diversity is the key; because the design industry needs illustration in so many ways. And while the advertising world offers bigger budgets, working with design agencies or direct with clients' in-house designers afford closer collaboration, with fewer hierarchies of "OKs" to get through.

Whether it's creating "Life Size Illustration" props for a window display at Top Shop, by Anna Lomax of Jiggery Pokery; a range of geometry-patterned hoodies for H&M Divided, by Siggi Eggertsson; inclusion in a limited-edition print portfolio commissioned by NB: Studio (and the four lucky illustrators were Anthony Burrill, Billie Jean, James Joyce and Paul Bowerl; drawing directly onto the walls of Zizzi restaurants up and down the country, in an illustration team that included Lizzie Marry Cullen, Camille Rousseau and Matthew Kavan Brooksl; or a long-running collaboration, such as between Angus Hyland of Pentagram and the luscious art materials retailer, Cass

Arts, using Marion Deuchars' distinctive hand-drawn typography to individuate their comprehensive product range – you must have seen those distinctive, buttercup yellow canvas totes emblazoned with "Young British Artist", swishing around town – it's all illustration in the service of design.

But that's just the tip of the iceberg; packaging, point-of-sale, vehicle livery, Christmas cards, wine labels, postage stamps, annual reports, letterheads and logos; every day a designer calls in the help of an illustrator, for all sorts of image-making opportunities. That's not to say, the designers aren't having a go at image-making too. Graphic designers have been encroaching on illustration's turf for a while now, especially since they figured out how to use Photoshop and Illustrator.

Far from retreating to their cosy studios and putting on the kettle, though, illustrators have been fighting back. Learning lessons from the design process, illustrators are instigating a whole host of projects. In the process, they're absorbing a bunch of new skills, and demonstrating to designers just

Feather Print by Danny Sangra
A Minute Silence Catalogue by Danny Sangra
Metronomy Video by Danny Sangra

i34 • Design • Essay

Liz Farrelly • Journalist, Editor, Curator and Broadcaster

want they're (potentially) missing.

Perhaps, some illustrators have been inspired by witnessing their work, applied to diverse products. "If Uniqlo in Tokyo and Beautiful Decay in Los Angeles, can put my image on a tee shirt, then why don't I, do-it-myself" goes the logic. For me, that can-do attitude has been the major revelation of the last year. Illustrators are still working in design, for consultancies, big and small, all over the country. But, they're also applying their images to their own products; combining illustration into designed objects, but on a smaller, more local scale, as one-offs, limited-editions and batches.

When Sanna Annukka has delivered her illustration for Marks & Spencers' Swiss Biscuit Collection, to be printed on a must-keep tin, she goes back to work on her own collections; limited-edition silk-screen prints, lithographs and a range of wooden, decorated "Soul Birds", which sell through her on-line shop. Bristling with folkloric references, and realised in intense jewel-like colours, Sanna's abstracted birds, animals and figures,

are modern-day icons, drawn from an age-old heritage.

Danny Sangra collaborates on commercial projects with art directors Harriman Steel, and fashion legend Marc Jacobs; but he also works with knitwear designer, Lynn Cockburn, on their own label, A Minute Silence. Inspired by wild geometry, bold colour palettes and a Mod sensibility, Danny uses his multiple-media skills to refine colour and pattern and promote and market these unique garments. He created the illustrations for the "look book" (based on retro knitting patterns) as well as a promo video, inspired by a 60s-style fashion shoot.

Emily Forgot is as happy working on a giant scale – creating murals and windows for Selfridges & Co – as she is scaling her alt-fairy-tale scenarios for limited-edition prints, selling at the on-line gallery, Thick & Thin. She also applies images to a range of ceramics, the Playground Plates; cleverly, the white background completes the one-colour prints.

Mixing high-profile commissions with her own obsessions; Kate Moross

worked with Start Creative to create a limited-edition print to celebrate Virgin Atlantic's 25th anniversary; next she's decorating a car for Vauxhall to promote their retro Roller Disco. Then she's designing record sleeves for her friends' bands and indie labels. Meanwhile, her range of clothes for Top Shop, and her limited-edition tees and jewellery, are hot sellers. Bold, primary colours, hand-rendered with extreme attitude, Kate's style is searingly contemporary, anti-elite, and a bit cute.

In 2009, Agathe Jacquillat and Tomi Vollauschek, of FL@33, rounded-up the very best products by illustrators, and some designers! The result; an awe-inspiring book, "Made & Sold: Toys, T-Shirts, Prints, Zines and Other Stuff". FL@33 are accomplished image-makers themselves; their inky, spindly figs feature animal and plant life, pattern and type. And, they're no strangers to the market place either; the partners also run Stereohype, a label and on-line store, featuring covetable garments, tees, badges, prints and postcards, produced in collaboration with a worldwide crew of fellow image-makers.

And although web commerce has been a crucial factor in the dissemination of many illustrators "own brands", you'll also find the best of these "did-it-myself" products in non-virtual stores, albeit, a little off the beaten track. Funnily enough, some of those unique emporia double as illustration galleries (Concrete Hermit), are run by designers (Shelf), and stock the very best books about illustration (Magma).

The symbiotic partnership between illustration and the design industry facilitates a diverse range of experiences. That illustrators have been inspired by their contact with commerce and taken the initiative, creating their own designed products, has resulted in some delicious "icing on the cake".

Playground Plates by Emily Forgot
Zoot Allure Window by Emily Forgot
Shoe Hoarding by Emily Forgot

M&S Tin by Sanna Annuka
Soul Birds by Sanna Annuka

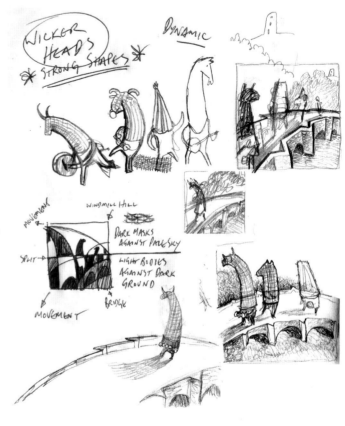

Jonathan McHugh has a strong sense of concept, composition and colour. He has illustrated for advertising, editorial, design and publishing clients in Germany, Japan, Dublin, London and Belfast. Numerous awards, including Gold at the Society of Artists' Agents Illustration Awards, London 2004. Jonathan lives beside an old windmill on the East coast of Ireland and surrounds himself with scraps of paper in an attempt to keep warm – sometimes he scribbles on them...

Medium Digital and mixed media
Brief 'Irelands Hidden Places' - image to depict a less well known place/aspect of Ireland/Irish folklore. Image/theme to maintain viewers interest for duration of month it will represent in the calendar.
Commissioned by
Richard Seabrooke and Brendan Byrne
Client Dynamo.ie
Commissioned for Allied Irish Bank

Based in Fife, Scotland, **Jill Calder** has been working as an illustrator since 1993 and combines traditional and digital methods to create her images. She is passionate about drawing, colour and teaching.

Although she loves her job, there are challenges: ropey clients, annoying art directors, copyright infringement and creative block... but these are all overshadowed by the wonderful variety that this job delivers!

"Garden Detectives" for National Museums Scotland was a real treat for Jill to work on, an experience enhanced by the enthusiastic team of designers and curators whose baby the project was. Because of the unusual nature of the project Jill feels that her excitement shows through in the illustration work - the Museum's visitors certainly responded very well to the exhibition!

Jill hopes that life as an illustrator continues to be as fun and creatively challenging as the last 17 years have been!

Medium Digital and mixed media
Brief One of several illustrations commissioned for 'Garden Detectives', an interactive and educational show aimed at children. This 8m x 2.2m wall image provided the lead into the exhibition space.
Commissioned by Maureen Barrie and Stuart Kerr
Client National Museums of Scotland

Garden Detectives need to keep their eyes and ears open!

i34 • Design • Bronze
Andy Potts • Audacious

Andy Potts is a London based illustrator and animator, originally from Kingswinford in the West Midlands. Since graduating with a BA Hons degree in illustration from Portsmouth in 95 his career has comprised image making, graphic design, animation and art direction. Over the last ten years the illustration work has taken centre stage and he has worked on numerous commissions with a wide variety of clients in advertising, book covers and editorial work for international newspapers and magazines including BBC, IBM, The Guardian and Time Out. His versatile style is a contemporary fusion of traditional and new techniques mixing hand crafted elements with digital collage and lots of colour.

Medium Digital and mixed media
Brief To create an energetic urban montage featuring various sports and activities that should induce a thirst for beer.
Commissioned by David Muro
Client Voicebox Creative
Commissioned for Pyramid Breweries

Gina Cross spent 10 years working
at the Guardian Newspaper,
commissioning illustration across all
sections of the paper. She continues
to work with illustrators by running
a print selling website 'A Little bit of
Art' and also works as a freelance
visiting lecturer to illustration courses
across the UK along with representing
illustrators as a freelance agent.
ginacross.co.uk

Editorial illustration still remains
relevant and important although it has
been hit hard by the recent budget
cuts in publishing. As the old cliché
of 'A picture paints a thousand words'
says, in the case of editorial illustration
it really is true. Illustration is used to
visually communicate discussions,
debates and concepts in a way that a
photograph cannot do. The importance
of editorial illustration is that it affords
the possibility of moving away from the
literal and offering something far more
interesting and less spoon-fed to the
reader. The function of an illustration
is to work in tandem with the headline
and attract the reader to the story –
draw them in, give them a feeling for
the piece and a desire to read it.

The experience I had of having
worked at the Guardian Newspaper
for nearly a decade, commissioning
illustration and assisting the art
directors in finding people to illustrate
the pages was a wonderful privilege,
and gave me and my colleagues
the opportunity to work with some
of the finest illustrators from all over
the world. I've had the chance to
select and commission illustrators
for heavy weight news pieces on
the Comment pages of the paper,
alongside commissioning for recipes,
relationships, drug addiction, Christmas
carols as well as more narrative pieces
to illustrate stories and concepts. The
art directors and designers continue
to commission inspired and inspiring
illustrators, who are selected on the
basis that there is no-one else that can
do that illustration!

Commissioning an illustrator for
a piece can be a strange affair. You
have a big pile of visual references
and bookmarks to illustrators' websites
and then a particular brief will come
in. From my own experience, quite
often I will mentally recall someone's
work and go looking for it, perhaps it
could have been untouched for a year,
while other times I have commissioned
people who are just exhibiting at the
D&AD show. What is always consistent
is the instinct that that person's style
is the right one for the piece, and it is
invariably a gut feeling – especially for
those with the very short deadlines.

Working as an editorial illustrator is
not for everyone. The tight deadlines

are certainly not for the faint-hearted.
For those that do relish a short
deadline, newspaper publishing is the
ultimate challenge. On an important
news day, many illustrators who have
worked on the comment pages of the
Guardian have not had finished copy
to work with and on occasion have
had to speak directly to the writer to
get the gist of the story – and then
have had only a couple of hours to
produce a finished piece of artwork.
That demands a mind that can grasp
the concept and visually communicate
it – as finished, perfect artwork in a
matter of hours.

The qualities that an illustrator
needs to demonstrate that they can rise
to that challenge is not only drawing
ability. It requires a point-of-view, an
attitude and understanding of what is
happening in the world. That is what
is transmitted to the viewer. Illustrators
I have spoken to often say that they
love the freedom of expression a short
deadline can give them – to not have
a prescribed brief as can often be the
case in commercial commissions, and
this allows them to really work at the
top of their game.

Some of the entrants in this year's
AOI Images have been working in
the field for many years. To mention
a few, Daniel Pudles stands out as
an example of a true professional
editorial illustrator, who always delivers
excellent artwork whatever the brief
– especially where political news is
concerned. Daniel is able to get right to
the essence of a brief, being politically
aware and concerned, he puts his heart
in to it. Ian Pollock is another who has
been at the forefront of character based
editorial illustration for many years, and
whose style is unmistakable.

Max Ellis has always managed to
straddle both worlds of advertising and
editorial illustration successfully – along
with other disciplines as he continues
to branch out into photography and
to experiment with different image
making techniques. What I admire
about Max's work is that he can turn
his hand to pretty much anything – he
is fearless, and quick too!

It's good to see Tobias Hickey
included here – he has a wonderful
ability to grasp concepts and produce
beautiful illustrations that are clearly

thought out and well executed.

There are many that are not
included whom are worth noting.
Joe Magee – who was awarded a
D&AD award in 2009 for Outstanding
Achievement – is an example of an
illustrator who continues to develop
his style and methods of working. You
get the sense from Joe's work that
he has gone in deep, responding to
each issue wholeheartedly. Matthew
Richardson is also very adept at
grasping concepts and turning them
into visually arresting images – his work
in editorial illustration and publishing is
accomplished and beautifully executed.

In features, there are some rising
stars too who have never been seen in
Images. A personal favourite of mine
has always been Helen Wakefield, who
rarely really promotes her work in a big
way but who never fails to come up
with a wonderful image imbued with
humour. Another personal favourite is
Demetrios Psillos, whose work I have
admired for years. He has the ability
to work quickly, produce wonderfully
complex coloured pieces, and grasp
characters in a unique way with a style
that can be applied to features and
narrative pieces too.

It would be great to see more work
by Paul Bommer, Paddy Molloy, Ben
Tallon, Sarah Lippett amongst others
in the years ahead, who manage to
combine working to tight deadlines
with unique styles and humour and
who succinctly grasp the requirements
for editorial commissions.

My concern for the current state
of publishing budgets is that there
are fewer outlets for the real talent
out there. The question is whether
animation will begin to feature more
strongly in editorial illustration as the
move towards digital media increases
for news stories and features, and
if newspapers and magazines are
going to be mostly online, do we need
static images anymore? I would say
yes, we do in this world that is moving
all the time – but equally, when used
in the right way, perhaps animated
images on features could add an extra
dimension to the articles. I just hope
that commissioners for online content
don't forget the value of editorial
illustration, as it is still relevant and
necessary in this digital age.

i34 · Editorial · Essay

Gina Cross · Artbuyer, Artist Representative and Curator

This conundrum that illustrators are facing presents them with other opportunities, for example the increase in self-publishing books – as with the recent launch and immediate success of Nobrow - providing a new outlet for their talent. Other illustrators are crossing the boundaries of being artists - using their skills to visually communicate in other ways, producing limited edition screen prints and giclees and putting on shows, forming collectives and clubs to enable their work to be seen.

Since my own recent departure from the Guardian, I am focusing on showing and selling graphic artwork – combined with teaching and mentoring illustration students to set them on the path of an illustrative career. I remain positive and hopeful for illustrators, and we are settling in to a new way of working with the technologies that seem to be currently threatening publishing and editorial illustration. The responsibility lies with the illustrators to enable themselves with the skills to compete, but I hope that art directors and editors don't overlook the potential for using editorial illustration in new ways.

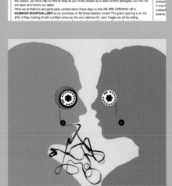

Royal Mail Strike by Demetrios Psillos
Mr NYT by Matthew Richardson
MP's Expense Scandal by Helen Wakefield
Coffee Without The Grind by Daniel Pudles
Duck With Fez On Scooter by Ian Pollock
Falling On Deaf Ears by Tobias Hickey
Website Blog at nobrow.net

Born in 1972 on the Isle of Wight, **James Fryer** feared a 'Wicker Man' style demise and so promptly swam the Solent to further his education. A Diploma and BA degree later he started out on his illustration career in 1995.

James's work is a blend of clever, innovative concepts and dramatic, atmospheric painting. This mix produces intelligent, thoughtful artwork that has been used in all major illustrative fields including advertising, publishing, design and editorial. Working predominantly for clients in the UK and US he has also had the pleasure of working for companies in France, Germany, Italy, Greece and Japan.

His many clients include Barclay's Bank, British Airways, BP, Royal Mail, BBC Worldwide, AMI, Home Office, Transport for London, Medical Defense Union, Unilever, Direct Line, King's College London, The Times, Telegraph, Independent, Financial Times, Times Educational Supplement, Times Higher Educational, Time Inc, Economist, New Statesman, Spectator, Prospect, New Scientist, Saga, Which?, Internazionale, Courier Japon, Marketing week, Design week, Future Publishing, Dennis Publishing, Duncan Baird Publishing.

James currently lives and works near the Hampshire / Surrey border.

Medium Acrylic
Brief Lifelong learning programmes across the country are closing due to government cuts. How is denying people a life changing second chance in any way fair?
Commissioned by Chris Barber
Client TSL Education Ltd
Commissioned for
Times Higher Education magazine

Peter Grundy and Tilly Northedge set up Grundy & Northedge in 1980 with information design as their mission. Firstly because it was a totally un-glamorous area of the business which they thought they could change, and secondly because it was less about selling things and more about explaining things, which seemed a lot more interesting.

When Tilly retired in 2006, Peter carried on the work renaming the studio 'GRUNDINI' with the intent of furthering the studios original mission of producing information design and illustration for clients who seek invention and imagination.

In fact the only really different thing today from the early years is that Peter uses an Apple computer rather than a geometry set.

Medium Digital
Brief This DPS diagram described the structure of the UK's professional development network of the teaching workforce.
Commissioned by Richard Doughty
Client The Guardian G2

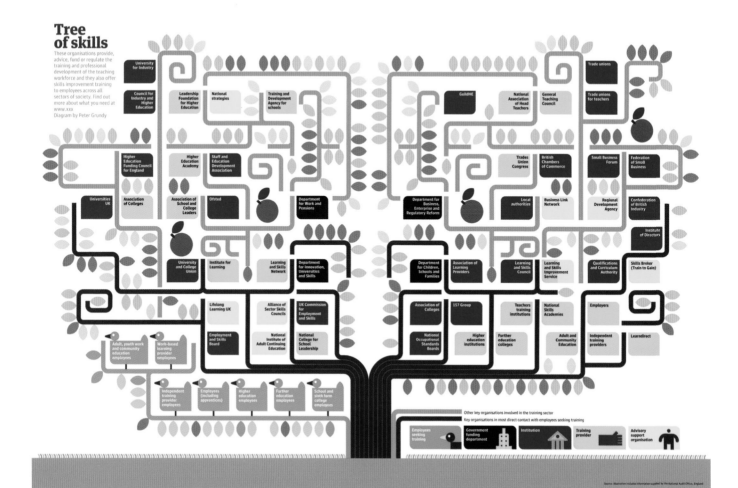

Tree of skills

These organisations provide, advice, fund or regulate the training and professional development of the teaching workforce and they also offer skills improvement training to employees across all sectors of society. Find out more about what you need at www.xxx
Diagram by Peter Grundy

i34 • Editorial • Bronze
Bill Butcher • Russia Resurgent

Bill Butcher was born in London and raised in Leigh-on-sea, Essex.

He graduated from Maidstone College of Art, which was the producer of many great illustrators, in the 1980's, then headed by Gerald Rose.

Bill has lived in Clerkenwell, London, for many years, where he works as a freelance illustrator for clients both in the UK and abroad.

His aim has always been to strive to make the idea the focus of the illustration to tell the story.

Aside to published work, Bill has recently been commissioned for both public and private portraits, such as the eminent Consultants of the Royal Free Hospital in Hampstead.

Medium Digital
Brief To illustrate in a political style the fact that Russia is now in a state of resurgence, and how the West should respond.
Commissioned by Penny Garrett
Client The Economist

i34 • New Media

Work commissioned for video, film and television; animation; character development and interactive design.

Editor, journalist and copywriter John O'Reilly has worked for clients including Virgin Atlantic, Getty Images, the British Council and Playstation. He was a regular contributor on art, music and media for The Guardian and Independent, an editor on Colors Magazine and The Modern Review. He writes visual trend reports and is the co-author of the recently published Recharge Your Design Batteries on commercial art and creativity. His Doctorate in Philosophy is from the University of Warwick, and has taught at several UK and European Universities on subjects ranging from psychoanalysis to Ferris Bueller to branding.

The New Stained Glass Window

The new back-lit portable iPhones and iPads and smartphones, herald a world of light and dark for illustrators. In one sense the future for illustration is dark. Not in the philosophical sense, though there will always be enough madness and insanity in the world for Ralph Steadman's imagery of fear and loathing. No, 'dark' in a warm, poetic way, the kind of 'dark' in Jorge Colombo's illustrations he creates on his iPhone for The New Yorker covers. The covers look the way they do partly because they have been exported from digital to print, the shiny paperstock can't quite replicate the backlit medium of the iPhone.

Colombo has three seemingly 'groundbreaking' technologies in his work. A new Apple iPhone; an application for the iPhone called Brushes, featuring an 'advanced colour picker' and several 'realistic brushes'; and a technology so advanced it has taken millions of years to fully evolve (or about 3,000 if you are a creationist) – his finger, which he draws with.

Out of the technology of his finger, Colombo generates a layer of washes, and dramatic chiaroscuro. And perhaps the greatest single contribution of the iPhone to illustration is that because it is backlit, it gives you enough light to draw at night. And like the iPhone illustrators will have a digital sketchbook to hand, that can immediately upload and distribute work. And while Colombo's work for The New Yorker is highly considered, these portable digital, networked, sketchpads give the illustrator an opportunity for reportage, on the spot editorial, in the moment. Colombo suspects technologies like this will be to drawing what email was for letter writing.

The ubiquity of photography from cameraphones has delivered lots of stories about citizen journalism, but few images that you would really call 'citizen journalism'. In the age of the amateur, professional photographers still take better photos. But reportage from illustrators can add editorial atmosphere and a sense of narrative storytelling to events. Think of Joe Sacco as a daily reporter. And there is also opportunity for new forms of illustrative documentary-making. Imagine if Ralph Steadman had been able to immediately upload on his travels with Hunter S. Thompson? (although probably only Steadman is disturbed enough to imagine it)

But the iPhone and iPad is also a medium of light. In an interview with Lawrence Weschler for The New York Review of Books, David Hockney highlights the immediacy of the iPhone as a painting tool. He always wanted to paint the dawn, but the lack of light to see the paints, or else the distorted light created by artificial light made it impossible. But now he can paint the dawn lying in bed, and as he points out, they lock into a unique illustration tradition, "the images always look better on the screen than on the page. "After all," says Hockney, "this is a medium of pure light, not ink or pigment, if anything more akin to a stained glass window than an illustration on paper."

Where new media technologies can really add value to illustrators, is the both disposability of the work, the sheer volume of images required to 'feed the beast', or the various new media beasts of internet, smartphones and iPads, and its 'originality', its uniqueness. As Lawrence Weschler remarks, the iPhone sketches Hockney sends to different friends are not, "second-generation digital copies of images that exist in some other medium: their digital expression constitutes the sole (albeit multiple) original of the image."

Smartphones and handheld devices are for diversion and entertainment. Rian Hughes who inspired a generation to explore the excitement of futurism through his work for 2000AD, collaborated with app developer Chilli X to create a time display for the iPhone. The thick black font of the hours and minutes contrast with the seconds display which fades over time – a minute. The best apps such as this, deliver a visual idea simply, and flatter the audience's taste. There's nothing like the buzz a reader gets from getting the joke or idea, that moment of comprehension delivered as visual thinking. But what all new media thrives on from social networking to amazon is personalization and customization. The Orange Mob Mates campaign used illustration to encourage users to create their own network, with each connected user being able to benefit from a cheap rate. Created by digital agency Poke, they enabled users to create their own mob mate social networking page, using illustrations to create characters to represent friends on the network. The idea is that the illustrator creates illustrations for others to use. And it's all simple shapes and bold colours, which is an advantage illustration has over photography in new media. And Poke again used this in their Balloonacy campaign for Orange, a balloon race across the internet. Grazing on new media really means responding to vibrant, simple shapes.

Likewise, Brendan Dawes' Doodlebuzz enables people to search for a news topic then draw/scribble a line which lays out the information for the user along whichever crazy line the

i34 • New Media • Essay

John O'Reilly • Journalist and Copywriter

user has drawn. Both of these point to the role of illustrator/designer as evangelist. They get people to use illustrations or think about how illustration is used to picture different kinds of information (how I see my friends/how the news agenda is normally arranged for me). In different ways both Orange Mob Mates and Doodlebuzz use illustration to help the user explore how communication happens. The most engaging illustration plays with the newness of the new media experience.

New Media is voracious, and between blogs, tweets and status updates, it doesn't do quiet very well. It makes attention seekers of us all, and encourages the idea that more communication is better communication. But what illustrators are expert at is cutting to the chase, capturing an idea in one simple image. Like Christoph Niemann's Abstract City Blog for The New York Times. It's not an extended self-promotion, or a blog about his opinions, or the work he likes, or his favourite pasta. It's short and simple, direct and funny. Life's too short for conventional blogging and tweeting. Have one idea, have fun, and prepared to be surprised at the attention you get.

One big new element of this shiny new experience is the quality of the imagery. As Hockney says, the screen is an opportunity to work with light, but it's also a chance to think in 3D, rotating imagery, animation. Most of all, those who succeed won't be intimidated by new media hyperbole of marketing and journalism, of 'cutting edge', 'breakthrough', 'groundbreaking'. The stained-glass window goes back to the 4th and 5th centuries. It's an old technology. The job of the 21st Century illustrators is to create different stains.

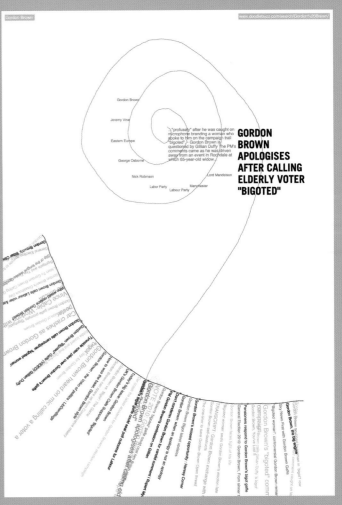

Chrysler New Yorker Cover by Jorge Colombo
Foodcart New Yorker Cover by Jorge Colombo

Doodlebuzz.com by Brendan Dawes

Orange Mob Mates Website by Poke London
Orange Baloonacy Website by Poke London

Steve May studied fine art painting and film-making in Nottingham. After touring with an unsuccessful pop band, he completed an MA in Animation at the Royal College of Art and currently works as a successful London based freelance illustrator and animation director.

Steve has worked widely in editorial, children's publishing and advertising. He illustrates a weekly column for The Guardian Guide. Steve has directed several short films including the award-winning GUT! and X & Y, which was nominated for the 2008 British Animation Awards. He has also worked extensively in TV and designed and directed Spacehopper Man for the acclaimed cult BBC series, Monkeydust.

Medium Digital
Brief Phantasmagorical sepia tinted creepfest with rabbits, ghouls and a cheeky nod to Ed D Wood. Go to youtube.com/watch?v=AO4A1Yyaa2o to see the whole animation.
Commissioned by Picasso Pictures

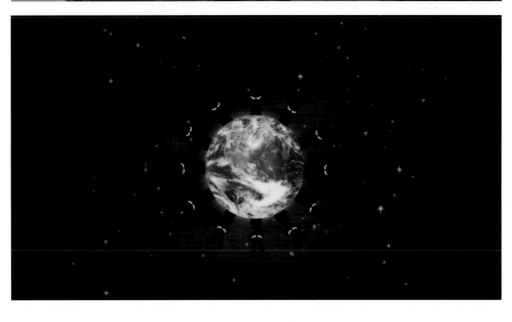

Action Stations is a collaborative motion graphics and art direction team set up by long time friends and colleagues Mark Taplin and Andy Potts. The aim is to generate striking work that utilises the best of their illustration/animation talents and to see what unexpected creative sparks fly when they literally knock their heads together. Their collective work experience covers most aspects of the visual media from advertising, publishing and editorial to tv, film and new media for a wide reaching international client base.

Medium Digital and mixed media
Brief To create an animated promo in response to the song 'Burn' integrating the band into an space themed narrative. Go to youtube.com/watch?v=Nf2tEtOv1bl to see the video.
Commissioned by Scuta Salamanca
Client The Dallas Guild

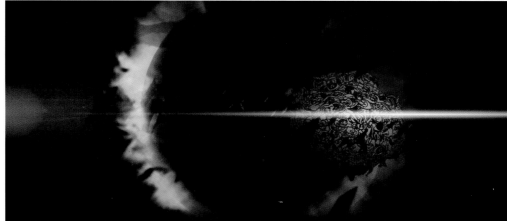

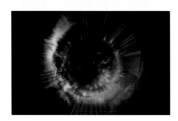

i34 • New Media • Bronze

Frances Castle • Primary History

Frances Castle has worked as a freelance illustrator since 2005 after beginning her career in the computer games industry.

Frances is inspired by comic book art and vintage children's books from the 50's and 60's, and loves good charity shop finds of old magazines, books and packaging. She is also a very keen historian and is currently illustrating a graphic novel documenting the search into her own Family Tree.

Frances has worked with a broad range of editorial and publishing clients including Readers Digest, The Guardian, BBC, Random House and Macmillan.

Medium Digital
Brief To produce illustrative timelines explaining different eras in history for primary school children. For use on their interactive website. Please explore the site: bbc.co.uk/schools/primaryhistory to see all of the illustrations.
Commissioned by Geoffrey Pais
Client BBC

Unpublished experimental work and personal promotional work, including speculative publishing projects and work rejected or not used by a client.

Jon Burgerman has built a strong reputation through his recognisable and colourful artworks of swooping, intertwining lines and hyper-emotional characters. Working across a variety of media that includes drawing, painting, print, animation, large scale murals and product design, his art retains a hand-made quality.

Burgerman exhibits internationally and has shown work alongside contemporary artists such as Banksy, Damien Hirst, Vivienne Westwood and Gerald Scarfe. His work is collected worldwide and is in the permanent collections of the V&A Museum and the Science Museum in London. He gives lectures, public performances and signings, and in late 2009 embarked on a pop music project as the band Anxieteam, who have played a series of worldwide gigs.

He has received two D&AD Silver award nominations and has collaborated with brands that include: Cadbury, Pepsi, Nike, Sony, Sky, Kidrobot, Nintendo, MTV, Levis amongst others. He also designed a special sick bag for Virgin Atlantic flights. In 2009 burger was setup to further explore brand collaborations and to manufacture his own product range.

Burgerman sometimes works in Nottingham and New York.

JonBurgerman.com

Self promotion is very important. If an artist paints a picture deep within a big forest does it make a sound, or more importantly, will anyone see it? Unless the local bears are looking to commission a few spot illustrations for their monthly periodical Creative Bearview, then probably not. Illustrators have a two-fold problem, making the work and then getting someone, somewhere to see it. There's so many everyday distractions (squirrels and shiny objects for instance) that sometimes it is very difficult for us to really see and take notice of anything. It's a tired cliche, but an apt one to plonk here, to stand out you need to offer something different. And good.

Maybe there is an issue in the way most illustrators think about self promotion? We want people to stand up and notice immediately, lunge over their desks for the phone, pushing everything off to one side, whilst frantically offering us a fat, juicy commission. 'Wow', they might say 'I just saw your postcard mailer, it blew my mind and I had to call immediately'. Maybe this does happen for some artists but I get the impression it's a rare occurrence.

I get a lot of emails from students. More often than not the question they really want answering (and the one I normally side step and try and avoid tackling) is 'how do you get your work out there ?'. Rarely does anyone ask 'how do I improve as an artist ?' or 'how do I have a quietly successful career that will sustain me well into my fifties?'. We are increasingly conditioned to want everything in the now, and then get disappointed when gratification isn't returned instantaneously. Often I stop myself replying to the student 'work out where?', do they know it can be lonely and cold out there? Knowing where the where is is pretty important. There's little point promoting your work in an arena unsympathetic to your style of work. 'Know your market' is a phrase I imagine a suited up marketing man might say.

As a recent graduate at the turn of the last decade I, for a short while, sent postcards to publishers, ad agencies and illustration agents. I kept a list of what I posted, who I sent it to and what their response was. The response was

generally universal, I heard back from no-one. Disheartened and worried about getting caught printing off postcards using the office printer at my then part-time job, I gave up actively self promoting. I reasoned that time would be better spent working on building a website and making new work for fun.

I sat in my little bedroom, on a cold metal fold up chair, and pottered around on my lethargic, beige PC. I cobbled together a website, teaching myself the odd bit of html and actionscript along the way. Once there was enough content on my site to entertain a weary eye, for a few moments at least, I decided to email people the link. The response was pretty much the same as the previous time but at least I actually heard back from some of the people. I now had their names to focus my disappointment and resentment towards.

Unbeknownst to me at the time, this was an important and significant turing point. I kept in touch with some of the contacts and over the years even have been commissioned by some of them. I'd gone from a faceless drone in a sea of millions of hungry artists to something almost approaching a real person. Yes, a real person with its own name and suggestion of a personality.

Successful self promotion, for me it seems, is a slow build. Sometimes it just takes time, for your work to develop and be appreciated and for the right kind of commissions to come along. 'Being in the right place, at the right time' is another dusty but true cliche, commonly spouted out by those who don't really want to say 'I was a bit lucky with my timing'.

The quick answer I offer those pesky, emailing students is to get a website. Make it yourself and put plenty of good work on it. If I had a website when I graduated a staggering, tear jerking, wrinkle inducing ten years ago (in an age of 56k dial up connections) then there's little excuse for Johnny Blackberry and Amelia iPhone not to have one today. Everyone has blogs, Facebook accounts and Flickr and all those social media time-black holes. Some people even have accounts setup for their pets. The first port of call should be to have a presence online. It's like a little digital shop window that

stays open 24/7, worldwide. Once that is done the next step is even easier, just fill it with great work.

Commissioners of great work want to know where to go to find the great work. Try and make it easy for them, they are probably busy people and like most people are easily distracted (those squirrels again). Whatever you produce and send out be sure to attach a little homing device to it (your URL), to lead inquisitive parties back to the source.

Actually making the great work is somewhat more tricksy but not completely impossible. The commissioners, as we've established, are easily distracted and lazy (I'm probably just projecting myself on to them here, apologies to all high-powered and dedicated commissioners reading this) and probably appreciate seeing, in context, how your illustration would work. It wasn't until I posted a picture of a wall mural on my website that I got commissioned to create more of them. That showed how my work would look scrawled haphazardly on an interior, and that it wasn't such an awful idea. Until then people would have had to imagine what my work might look like on a wall. Before that they first would have needed to conceive the initial idea of a mural. That's a lot of imagining, and imagining takes up valuable brain energy.

It is great to work for 'real' clients but if you're a little scant on client work this shouldn't be a barrier, or excuse, for not having anything in your portfolio or on your website. A lecturer once told me, during the interview process to get onto the art course I was applying to, that to save a lot of time they should just weigh each applicants folder. Heavy ones, with lots of work in would often mean the potential student was indeed proactive, hard working and studious. I made a mental note to only use heavy weight stock for my portfolio from then on.

Self directed work is what I always return to when not being harangued by clients or my parents (to visit them, they've never commissioned me). I don't purposefully make work for myself to gain commercial commissions. I try and keep my personal work pure and untainted, the decadence of art for the sake of art. The self directed work is usually unusual and sometimes has a

i34 • Self Promotion • Essay
Jon Burgerman • Artist and Illustrator

little tale behind its origins. A story or a small point of interest (for example, here's a book I made with an artist from another country that I've never met or spoken to) that marks the project out from the norm will only help generate attention towards it.

It's in the unnecessary, arbitrary play of self directed work were we can experiment without fear of failure or client disapproval, were perhaps the unexpected development and growth of the work might take place. And if you stick these shining examples of New and Exciting and Different (let's give it the acronym of NED) on your website and mailers then who knows, it might spark off an idea in a commissioners brain that will have them urgently lunging towards the phone to speak to you about a job.

Concrete Tag Show
An early hand painted installation at Concrete in Amsterdam.

Pens Are My Friends
300+ page monograph published by IdN. Designed by Unthink.

Burger Products
Products designed and manufactured by burger.

Heroes Of Burgertown
3 inch vinyl figures, produced by Kidrobot.

Characters
Digital characters. First made into a poster and then used for various products such as the laptop sleeves and wrapping paper.

Stickers
Diecut character stickers, sold and used as promotional give-aways.

Stuart McReath is a conceptual illustrator from the United Kingdom. He graduated from Leeds University in 1996 with a BA Hons Degree in Graphic Design where he specialised in Illustration. His clients have included many magazines, book publishers and advertising agencies and his original paintings are located in private and corporate collections around the world.

After working as an illustrator for several years, Stuart changed his artistic direction towards design. However, yearning to illustrate again, he has recently returned with passion and a concentrated focus on producing thought provoking conceptual illustrations.

Medium Acrylic
Brief The potential risks for writers and journalists in contemporary society.

Olivier Kugler was born in Stuttgart, Germany, grew up in a small village in the Black Forest, and was influenced by French/Belgian bande desinées and Otto Dix. After military service in the Navy he studied graphic design in Pforzheim and worked as a designer in Karlsruhe for a few years. He got terribly bored with it and received a scholarship from the German Academic Exchange Service to do a Masters in illustration at the School of Visual Arts in New York. Since then he's worked as an illustrator in London for clients all over the world.

Olivier has a special interest in reportage illustration, drawing inspiration from the people he meets and the places he visits. He draws on location and from his own reference photos.

Medium Digital and mixed media
Brief One of a larger series of spreads documenting places I visited and people I met whilst travelling through Iran.

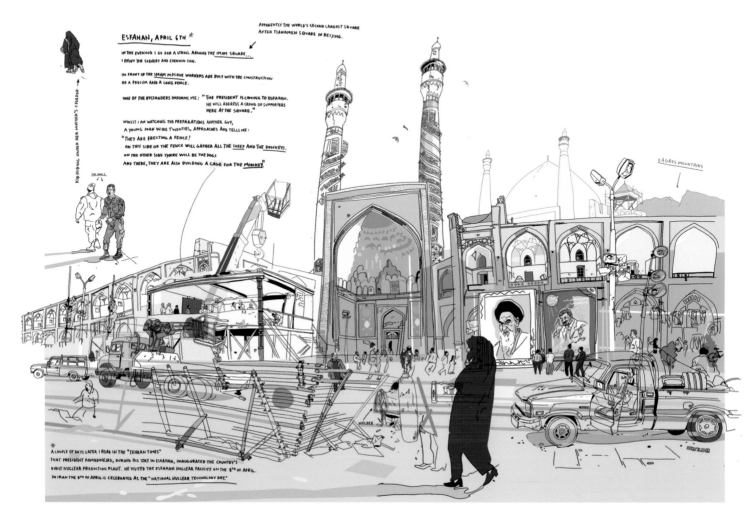

i34 • Self Promotion • Bronze

Ian Henderson • Domestication Run

Ian Henderson is an illustrator based in London, where he came to study book illustration many years ago. He works in a hand drawn style using pencil, markers or pen and ink and often incorporates decorative elements into the design.

His influences come out in several pieces, carrying elements of 'gothic' or surreal imagery (hopefully in not too clichéd a manner) and with roots in old film, myth and folk-tales.

Apart from published work, he has occasionally exhibited in galleries in London and the surrounding area.

Recent work includes a set of drawings for Stravinsky's musical play 'The Soldier's Tale' and an illustrated book project.

Medium Pencil
Brief A visual representation of the domestication of animals, portrayed by their transfer from wild habitat to tamed environment via a human agent.

Each entry is marked by the jury
according to how well the work fulfils
the brief, originality, and technical
ability. Only the highest scoring images
are invited to feature in the annual.

Victoria Topping
Cockerel
Category Self Promotion
Medium Digital and mixed media
Brief This was the first in a series of bird illustrations I created for a exhibition I had at the Nature in Art Museum in Gloucestershire.

Garry Parsons
National Moth Night
Category Self Promotion
Medium Digital and mixed media
Brief Britain's celebration of moths and moth recording. Join in the fun and marvel at the beauty.

Wrestling With Your Finances
Category Self Promotion
Medium Digital and mixed media
Brief In the downturn your financial worries can loom large.

From The Beginning
Category Editorial
Medium Digital and mixed media
Brief Running for beginners! Start running today and reap the benefits immediately.
Commissioned by Russell Fairbrother
Client Natmag-Rodale
Commissioned for Runner's World Magazine

Garry Parsons
George's Cosmic Treasure Hunt
Category Children's Books
Medium Mixed media
Brief Cover illustration with integrated interior
illustrations. Unique book, combining both a
narrative storyline with educational non-fiction.
Commissioned by James Fraser
Client Random House Children's Books

Angela Morelli
The Steady State Economy
Category Design
Medium Digital
Brief The Steady State Economy project, based
on article published in the New Scientist,
is a friendly info-graphic representation of
eco-economist Herman Daly's work on a
sustainable economic system.
Commissioned by Jody Boehnert
Client Eco-Labs.org

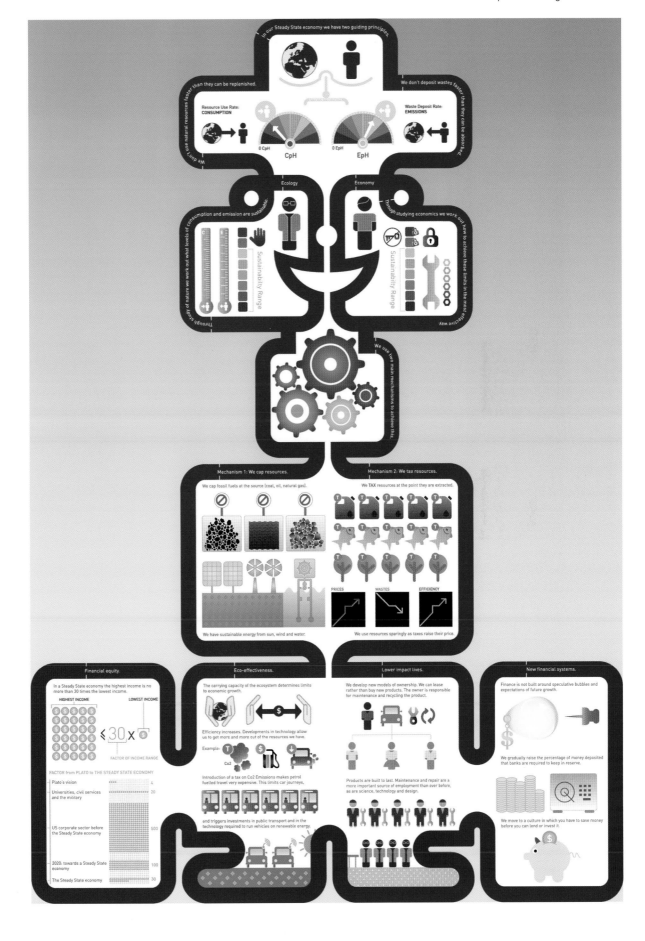

Sebastien Braun
Ralph Loved Picture Books (Very Much)
Category Self Promotion
Medium Mixed media
Brief Experimental work.

Meeow And The Little Chairs
Category Children's Books
Medium Digital
Brief Picture book for 2-3 yrs. The lead character, Meeow, initiates play situations with his friends. They create and imagine fun games with simple objects. The final image reveals what they imagine.
Commissioned by David Bennett
Client Boxer Books

Alexis Goodwin
Off To Buy Potatoes!
Category Self Promotion
Medium Digital and mixed media
Brief Fourth image taken from 'Greedy Pig' a self
authored and illustrated story book. The story
tells of the influence of an accident insurance
salesman who arrives in a small Victorian town.

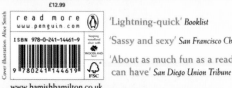

'Lightning-quick' *Booklist*

'Sassy and sexy' *San Francisco Chronicle*

'About as much fun as a reader can have' *San Diego Union Tribune*

£12.99

read more
www.penguin.com

ISBN 978-0-241-14461-9

9 780241 144619

www.hamishhamilton.co.uk

Cover illustration: Alice Smith

REVENGE OF THE
MOONCAKE VIXEN
MARILYN CHIN

Marilyn Chin
A MANIFESTO IN 41 TALES
REVENGE OF THE
MOONCAKE VIXEN

Anna Higgie
Vienna
Category Self Promotion
Medium Pencil
Brief Select a city that you find inspiring and that connects well with your style. Content: anything you like, as iconic or as general as you want, as long as it relates to the city you have chosen.

Alice Smith
Revenge Of The Mooncake Vixen
Category Books
Medium Collage
Brief To design a surreal, colourful book cover that references classical Chinese tales and 20th century American culture.
Commissioned by John Hamilton
Client Hamish Hamilton / Penguin

Lee Woodgate
Darwin
Category Self Promotion
Medium Digital and mixed media
Brief Create a portrait for self-promotional mail shot.

Tesla
Category Self Promotion
Medium Digital
Brief Illustration for a self initiated series
of portraits of pioneers in science.

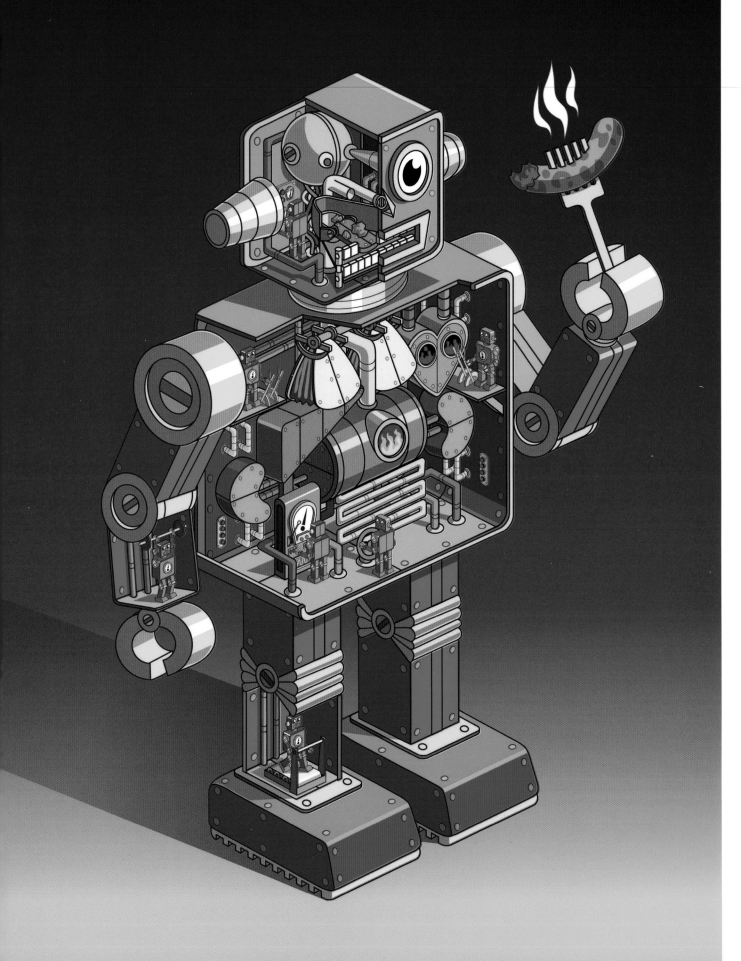

Rod Hunt
Measuring Metabolism
Category Editorial
Medium Digital
Brief Create a robot image so that you can view
into the inside of the body seeing the mechanics
of the metabolism.
Commissioned by Hilary Fitch
Client Sobefit Magazine

Chessington World Of Adventures
Theme Park Map
Category Design
Medium Digital
Brief Create an accurate and easy navigation
tool for visitors, that's colourful, fun and appealing
to the target family audience.
Commissioned by
Karis Galliano / David Johnstone
Client LMC Design
Commissioned for
Chessington World of Adventures

Rod Hunt
Where's Stig? Deep South Adventure
Category Books
Medium Digital
Brief "Find the mysterious Stig, Top Gear's
resident racing driver." Recreate the Deep South
Adventure episode of the TV Show Top Gear for
the new book "Where's Stig?".
Commissioned by Charlie Turner
Client Top Gear / BBC Books

Where's Stig? In Tokyo
Category Books
Medium Digital
Brief "Find the mysterious Stig, Top Gear's
resident racing driver." Create a Tokyo scene
based on the Japan Race episode of the TV
Show Top Gear for the new book "Where's Stig?".
Commissioned by Charlie Turner
Client Top Gear / BBC Books

Where's Stig? Botswana Adventure
Category Books
Medium Digital
Brief "Find the mysterious Stig, Top Gear's
resident racing driver." Recreate the Botswana
Adventure episode of the TV Show Top Gear for
the new book "Where's Stig?".
Commissioned by Charlie Turner
Client Top Gear / BBC Books

Fishy Sub
Category Self Promotion
Medium Digital
Brief Create a new piece for the group show
Hot Rods & Hairy Beasts.

Jonathan Burton
Lucknam Park
Category Editorial
Medium Pencil, Digital
Brief To illustrate the Giles Coren restaurant review for Lucknam Park. The German waiters and 40's style decor gave the reviewer the sensation of stepping into a wartime adventure film.
Commissioned by Chris Hitchcock
Client The Times

The Quest For The Tasmanian Tiger
Category Editorial
Medium Ink, pencil, collage, 3D, photography, digital
Brief The Tasmanian Tiger has thought to be extinct since the 1920's but recent apparent sightings have bought a new interest and a race to find if the animal still exists...
Commissioned by Martin Colyer
Client Readers Digest Magazine

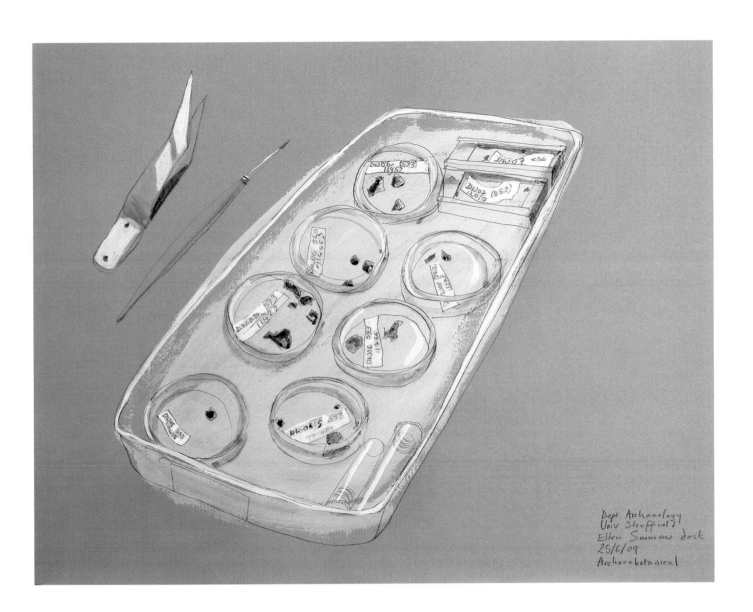

Julia Midgley
Ellen's Desk
Category Self Promotion
Medium Acrylic, acrylic ink, and pencil
Brief To document with drawing the Post
Excavation Analysis of finds from the Stonehenge
Riverside Project 2009.
Commissioned by Dr. Helen Wickstead
Client Artists+Archaeology

Lucy Davey
Mud, Muck And Dead Things
Category Books
Medium Digital and mixed media
Brief To create a cover for the crime novel Mud,
Muck and Dead Things, set in the Cotswolds.
Commissioned by Wendy Birch
Client Headline

Murder On The Orient Express
Category Books
Medium Digital and mixed media
Brief To create a cover for Agatha Christie's
Murder on the Orient Express.
Commissioned by Sirida Pensri
Client Pearson Education
Commissioned for Penguin Readers

Willi Gray
Fundamentalism
Category Self Promotion
Medium Digital and mixed media
Brief The impact of Christian
fundamentalism on the American psyche.

Satoshi Kambayashi
Die Fledermaus
Category Self Promotion
Medium Digital and mixed media
Brief Poster for Johann Strauss Jr's
comic operetta, Die Fledermaus,
featuring (Adele's) Laughing Song.

Nightmare On Wall Street
Category Editorial
Medium Digital and mixed media
Brief The credit crunch has turned into
a bloodbath on Wall Street. (Article
written at the height of disaster
unfolding, September 2008).
Commissioned by Una Corrigan
Client The Economist

Feeding Time For Germany
Category Editorial
Medium Digital and mixed media
Brief Germany cannot keep relying on
domestic consumption alone for its
economic growth.
Commissioned by Una Corrigan
Client The Economist

Email Security
Category Editorial
Medium Digital and mixed media
Brief Can emails be made more
secure through various methods
including Public-key cryptography?
Commissioned by John-Henry Barac
Client The Guardian

Satoshi Kambayashi

Mayor Boris Finishes His First Year
Category Editorial
Medium Digital and mixed media
Brief Boris Johnson has successfully
completed his first year as mayor of London,
and is quite popular.
Commissioned by Andrew Tod
Client The Guardian

The Tank Man Of Culture War
Category Editorial
Medium Digital and mixed media
Brief People in China are beginning to take
stand against the government's destruction
of cultural heritage in the name of progress.
Commissioned by Andrew Tod
Client The Guardian

Folly in The Sand
Category Editorial
Medium Digital and mixed media
Brief Dubai's property development would be
reclaimed by the desert.
Commissioned by Andrew Tod
Client The Guardian

Christmas Books
Category Editorial
Medium Digital and mixed media
Brief Create a near full page illustration for
the 'Books for Christmas' feature.
Commissioned by David Gibbons
Client New Statesman

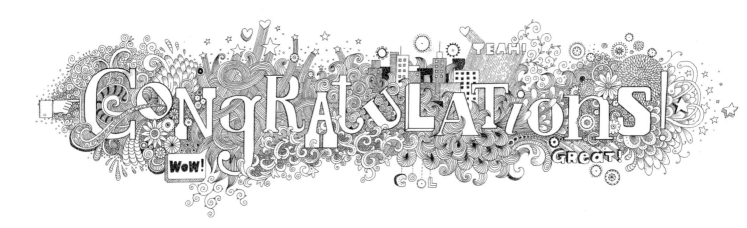

James Gray
Congratulations
Category Design
Medium Ink
Brief Design a celebratory greeting card
using lettering and pattern.
Commissioned by Hallmark

Russell Wilson
In Dock
Category Design
Medium Mixed media
Brief Contemporary male design for greeting card.
Commissioned by Hallmark

Elaine Hughes
Holly
Category Design
Medium Mixed media
Brief Mystical figurative work based on
Xmas trends for greeting cards.
Commissioned by Hallmark

Simon Pemberton
Songlines - Bruce Chatwin
Category Books
Medium Mixed media
Brief To create a simple bold image that captures
the heat and wide open spaces of the Australian
aboriginal landscape and a sense of Chatwin's
travels across it.
Commissioned by Sheri Gee
Client The Folio Society

Snowstorm
Category Self Promotion
Medium Mixed media
Brief Take a light hearted look at our
obsession with TV at Christmas. We'll
watch it anywhere any time.

Geoffrey Fisher
1939-1945

Kenneth Andersson
Jeffrey Fisher
Category Design
Medium Digital and mixed media
Brief One of 10 postcards in box to promote Black
Sun Group and their new studio, situated in the
old country residence of the Bishops of London.
Commissioned by Paul Edison
Client Black Sun Studio

Robot (The Rocket Science Series)
Category Self Promotion
Medium Digital and mixed media
Brief One of 12 posters.

Clouds (The Rocket Science Series)
Category Self Promotion
Medium Digital and mixed media
Brief One of 12 posters.

Tree
Category Self Promotion
Medium Digital and mixed media
Brief Personal project.

Good Wives and Warriors
Swatch/Manish Arora Advertising Campaign
Category Advertising
Medium Fineliner, felt-pen and digital
Brief To create an international advertising campaign for the Manish Arora/Swatch watch collection.
Commissioned by Florian Gruetzner
Client Swatch/Manish Arora

Yulia Brodskaya
Cadbury
Category Advertising
Medium Paper and card
Brief Capture the journey of a glass and a
half of milk into a bar of chocolate. The aim is
to communicate Cadbury Dairy Milk's quality
and craft, including the fact that it is made
with real milk content.
Commissioned by Keith Doyle
Client Publicis QMP
Commissioned for Cadbury

Antony Cattini
Origin
Category Self Promotion
Medium Digital and mixed media
Brief An illustration depicting the origin of
knowledge, good and evil. The Serpent is sent to
persuade Eve to eat from the Tree of Knowledge.
The contrast between light and shadow
represents good and evil.

Polly Horner
Grandpa And The Stars
Category Self Promotion
Medium Watercolour
Brief One page from the children's book 'Goodbye
Grandpa' which is as yet uncommissioned.

Paul Blow
Perfectionism
Category Editorial
Medium Digital and mixed media
Brief Illustration for the front cover of the Boston
Globe magazine. "When Perfectionism Becomes
a Problem".
Commissioned by Chin Wang
Client Boston Globe Magazine

Skeel Bros
Category Editorial
Medium Digital and mixed media
Brief Illustrate the narrative recalling the Great
Depression and one family's shame at having
to pawn their possessions to survive.
Commissioned by Alex Breuer
Client Times T2

Eri Griffin
Sailing
Category Design
Medium Ink
Brief One of the series of Cazenove Capital
Management re-branding illustrations. New
brand illustrations include Architectures, Flower,
Animals, Music scene and Sports scene.
Commissioned by Phillip Moore
Client Cazenove Capital Management

Black Bird And White Bird
Category Self Promotion
Medium Ink
Brief One of the cover design concept of "A Folio
Anthology of Poetry". This book was published by
The Folio Society in late 2009, cover and interior
illustrations by Eri Griffin.

Time
Category Self Promotion
Medium Ink
Brief One of the cover design concept of
"A Folio Anthology of Poetry". This book was
published by The Folio Society in late 2009,
cover and interior illustrations by Eri Griffin.

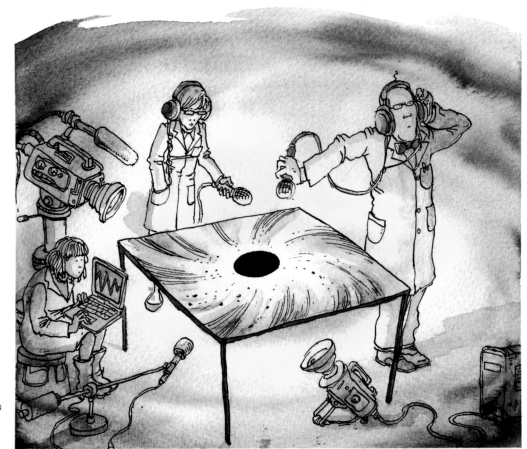

David Simonds
Local Government Is Broke
Category Editorial
Medium Watercolour
Brief Illustrate article about the deteriorating
state of local government services.
Commissioned by Una Corrigan
Client The Economist

Desktop Black Holes
Category Editorial
Medium Watercolour
Brief Illustrate for science section article describing
an experiment to emulate sound waves given off
by black holes on laboratory worktop.
Commissioned by Una Corrigan
Client The Economist

Jan Bowman
This Is Birmingham:
A Glimpse Of The City's Secret Treasures
Category Children's Books
Medium Digital
Brief Inspired by Miroslav Sasek's *This is...* books.
A history of the Lunar Society (18th-century
scientists and freethinkers who kickstarted the
Industrial Revolution), describing how Birmingham
was built by immigrants; also illustrates beautiful
parts of the city omitted in tourist guides.
Written and illustrated by Jan Bowman.
Commissioned by Ron Grosset
Client Waverley Books

We realise
parenting
can be tough

So we've made
buying life insurance
the easy part

**Life Insurance
from Aviva**

Get a quote ▶

Get a quote ▶

Vicky Woodgate
Aviva Life Insurance - Loved Ones
Category Advertising
Medium Digital
Brief Part of an animated web banner campaign I
created for Aviva loved ones - life Insurance. A child
having a tantrum, with her in a huff at the end.
Commissioned by Deborah Parkinson
Client Chemistry Agency
Commissioned for AVIVA

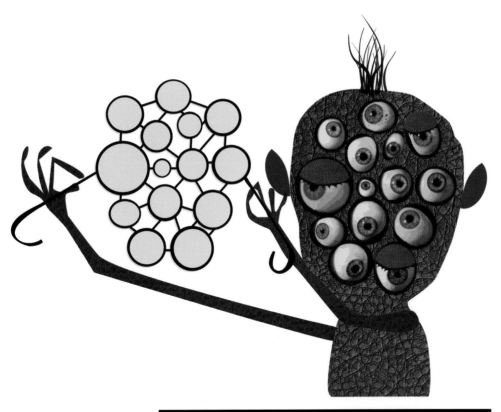

Claire J Senior
Adapt
Category Self Promotion
Medium Digital and mixed media
Brief Open brief to create an image
pertaining to the topic: adapt.

Noah's Ark
Category Self Promotion
Medium Digital and mixed media
Brief To create an engaging and visually
rich illustration using the textures and
shapes of everyday objects.

Laura Scott
The Piano-tuner
Category Self Promotion
Medium Ink, acrylic and digital
Brief Produce a series of illustrations in response
to reading Angela Carter's 'The Bloody Chamber'.

Christopher Harper
Wrestling With Angels
Category Self Promotion
Medium Digital and mixed media
Brief To create an illustrative response to the
Genesis narrative of Jacob and the Angel.

<

Femke de Jong
Sustainability
Category Self Promotion
Medium Digital and mixed media
Brief The idea came from the 'sustainable'
environment of a heart-lung machine,
similar to our situation on earth.

Jake Abrams
Plug'ole
Category Editorial
Medium Pen and Ink- Digital
Brief Cover illustration for editorial on
'Pulling the Plug on the G20'.
Commissioned by Clice Crook
Client The Spectator

Cutting
Category Editorial
Medium Pen and Ink- Digital
Brief Editorial comment piece on how the major
political parties approach public spending cuts.
Commissioned by Clice Crook
Client The Spectator

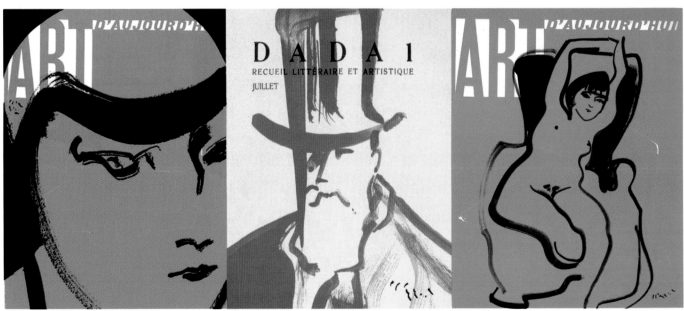

PITTSBURGH **OPERA**
FALSTAFF

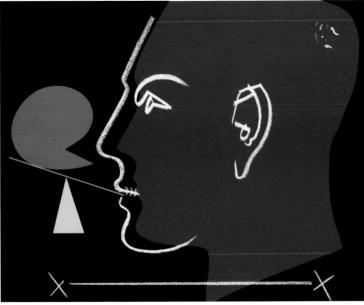

Brian Grimwood
Liberty
Category Editorial
Medium Digital and mixed media
Brief New Liberty.

Grimwood Postcard
Category Self Promotion
Medium Digital and mixed media
Brief Self-promotional work.

Falstaff
Category Advertising
Medium Digital and mixed media
Brief Poster for Falstaff ...one of a series
of five productions.
Commissioned by Daniele Caruso
Client MARC USA
Commissioned for Pittsburgh Opera

Conversation
Category Editorial
Medium Digital and mixed media
Brief Establish clear ground rules about keeping
any personal stories anonymous and the extent
of confidentiality to create a safe environment.
Commissioned by Dan Sinclair
Client TES Education Ltd

Black Coffee Project
Hope!
Category Self Promotion
Medium Digital and mixed media
Brief To show that children offer us a
chance to change the future of our planet
and that nature will always find a way.

The Massive Rat
Category Editorial
Medium Digital and mixed media
Brief To Illustrate David Mitchell's
short story about one man's failing
marriage and his struggle with life. The
illustration needed to be "quite dark and
atmospheric and a bit mysterious".
Commissioned by
Pauline Doyle / Maggie Murphy
Client The Guardian Weekend

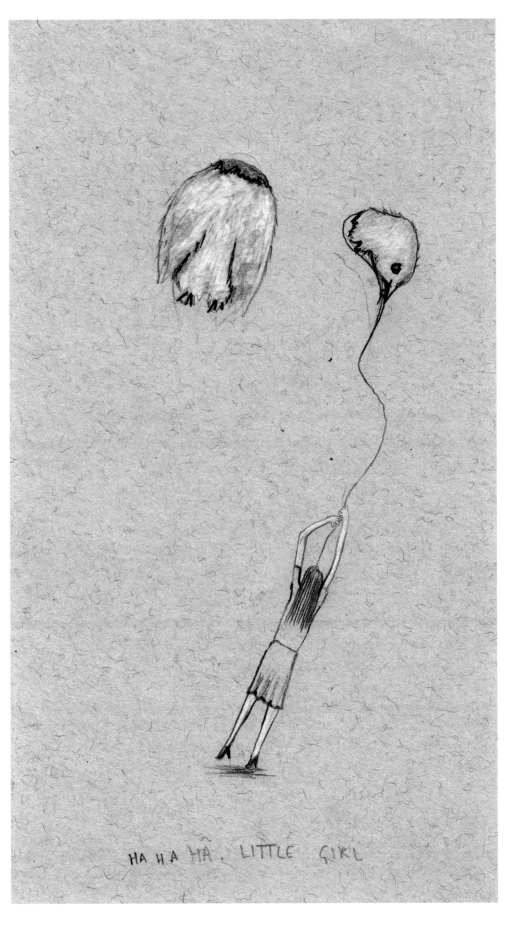

HA HA HA. LITTLE GIRL

Laura J Frame
I Can't Catch
Category Self Promotion
Medium Pencil
Brief Personal work referring to the danger of not knowing when to revere certain people only from afar. Sometimes they can only retain their essence and be who they were as they wander untamed.

Erika Pal
Azad's Camel – The City – The Race – The Desert
Category Children's Books
Medium Mixed media
Brief A 40 page picture book for children aged 5-7.
Set in the Middle East, a boy reluctantly becomes
a camel jockey, but befriends his camel and they
escape to the desert together.
Commissioned by Judith Escreet
Client Frances Lincoln Publishers

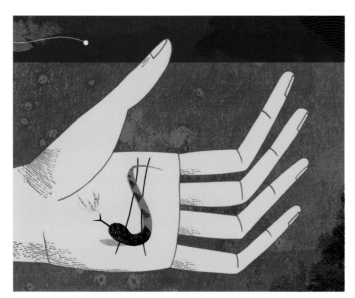

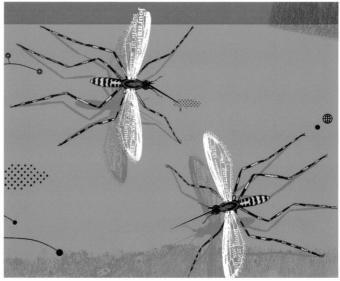

Frazer Hudson
Corrupt Giveaway
Category Editorial
Medium Digital and mixed media
Brief Depict the corrupt nature of the
American monetary system including
government handouts during the
credit crunch crisis.
Commissioned by Gina Cross
Client The Guardian
Commissioned for
Comment & Debate section

Blood Suckers
Category Editorial
Medium Digital and mixed media
Brief The illustration should depict
journalists as irritating, annoying pests.
Commissioned by Gina Cross
Client The Guardian
Commissioned for
Comment & Debate section

Kimberley Pope
I Dream Of Nimbostratus...
Category Self Promotion
Medium Digital
Brief To self: must be good
and develop my black and
white portfolio.

Feilo
Libido
Category Self Promotion
Medium Digital
Brief Promotional piece exploring the
darker side of one's psyche and libido.

The Escape
Category Self Promotion
Medium Digital
Brief Promotional piece exploring the
struggle to escape dark, negative forces.

Ned Jolliffe
Turning 50
Category Editorial
Medium Digital
Brief To illustrate the 'happiness curve'. Often
we experience a lifetime 'low' on turning 50, but
at 80 we often return to being as happy as we
were at 20!
Commissioned by Jon Stock
Client Daily Telegraph Weekend

Jonathan Gibbs
Back To Earth
Category Design
Medium Wood engraving
Brief To illustrate growth and industry for an
investment management conference.
Commissioned by Edward Hocknell
Client Baillie Gifford

The Saltyard
Category New Media
Medium Wood engraving
Brief To illustrate an image of a coastal landscape
with agriculture and nature. 'Water, salt marsh,
fish, big sky, birds... hints at food and feasting
without being too specific'.
Commissioned by Elizabeth Hallett
Client Hodder and Stoughton
Commissioned for Saltyard Book co.

Mark Hearld Bookplate
Category Design
Medium Wood engraving
Brief To design a bookplate for artist Mark Hearld,
to be printed directly from the block.
Commissioned by Mark Hearld

Belle Mellor
The Coming Jobs Crisis
Category Editorial
Medium Digital, pen and ink
Brief Cover image illustrating the imminent
dangers of mass unemployment posed to
workers everywhere.
Commissioned by Graeme James
Client The Economist

**There Is No Concealing Pregnancy From
The Midwife**
Category Self Promotion
Medium Digital, pen and ink
Brief 'There is no concealing pregnancy from the
midwife'. One of a set of illustrations produced for
a booklet of proverbs from around the world.

Never Judge A Book By Its Cover
Category Self Promotion
Medium Digital, pen and ink
Brief Cover and endpaper illustration produced for
a booklet of proverbs from around the world.

<

Zara Slattery
Mistress Pate Sitting In The Lychgate
Category Children's Books
Medium Acrylic ink and Gouache
Brief To illustrate an Elizabethan Picture book
with full colour and b&w illustrations for children,
7-10 year olds. To integrate ideas produced in
child and family workshops.
Commissioned by Lisa Rigg
Client Hackney Historic Buildings Trust

Max Pepe
Euphoria
Category Self Promotion
Medium Digital and mixed media
Brief One of a selection of illustrations on
the subject of 'The Madness of Love'.

Vic Turnbull
The Truffle Shuffle
Category Self Promotion
Medium Scraperboard and digital media
Brief Self-promotional.

The Cow Jumped Over The Moon
Category Self Promotion
Medium Scraperboard
Brief Self-promotional.

Patrick Regout
Hulot Tango
Category Self Promotion
Medium Digital
Brief To pay tribute to the movie "Mon Oncle" by French director Jacques Tati. The image was showed at the exhibition "Tati and Friends" at the Seed Factory (Brussels).

Later I understood what seized my IMAGINATION that day

HOW STRANGE IT WAS TO SEE MEN DO SOMETHING BEAUTIFUL

SUBSCRIBER
More paper for your money
theguardian TheObserver

Andy Smith
Breathe
Category Advertising
Medium Digital
Brief Illustrate the quote provided taken
from the surfing novel 'Breathe' published
by Picador. Use one colour only.
Commissioned by Alex Bec
Client Hudson Bec
Commissioned for Picador/Foyles Bookshop

Subscription Crowd
Category Advertising
Medium Digital
Brief Illustrate a large varied crowd of figures
who may subscribe to The Guardian newspaper.
Commissioned by Giles Brenard
Client The Guardian

Read Em And Weep
Category Editorial
Medium Digital
Brief Illustrate the over elaborate,
confusing language used in restaurant
menus using decorative lettering.
Commissioned by Meg Georgeson
Client Squaremeal Magazine

Fiammetta Dogi
Grey Whale
Category Editorial
Medium Acrylic
Brief To illustrate a Grey Whale with an
inset demonstrating how the whale feeds
on the sea floor. The style required was
cut-to-white, realistic but painterly.
Commissioned by Mishka Westell
Client BBC Magazines: Wildlife

Alison Jay
The Owl And The Pussycat
Category Children's Books
Medium Alkyd on paper with varnish
Brief Illustrate a book of nursery rhymes
with linking back story. Brief fairly open.
Commissioned by Libby Hamilton
Client Templar Publishing

Reading Bee
Category Children's Books
Medium Alkyd on paper with varnish
Brief An illustration for a company that produce
prints on canvas for children's bed rooms.
Commissioned by Mia Papania
Client Happy Spaces
Commissioned for Happy Spaces

Alice Melvin
Seventeen Starlings
Category Children's Books
Medium Screenprint
Brief Illustrate: 'As day turns to dusk and the sun starts to set, seventeen starlings are not asleep yet. Up on the chimneys they noisily chat, safe from the claws of the tortoiseshell cat.'
Commissioned by Tate Publishing

Toby Whitebread
Rollercoaster
Category Editorial
Medium Digital and mixed media
Brief To illustrate a magazine article about the
Charlatans frontman, Tim Burgess. I was given
the text of the interview and then asked to
come up with supporting illustrations.
Commissioned by Angel Greenham
Client Subvert Magazine

Classic Hitch
Category Self Promotion
Medium Digital and mixed media
Brief A tribute to the master of suspense.

David Bray
Flower
Category Self Promotion
Medium Ink
Brief It's a self-initiated project, after my girlfriend said she had tasted the sweetest honey she had ever tasted.

Richard Fairhead
Characters
Category Self Promotion
Medium Digital and mixed media
Brief This is a collection of commissioned and personal work from the last year. It's includes various creations including The Prawn Cowboy, and Chewee sporting a tracksuit. Everyone's a winner...

Christine Berrie
19 Cameras
Category Self Promotion
Medium Pencil
Brief A study of vintage cameras I have collected over the years.

Stephen Walter
Liverpool 08-09
Category Self Promotion
Medium Pencil
Brief A vast project intended
to map out Liverpool through
personal experiences, locals'
knowledge and insights, and
research from the internet and
cultural and historical books.

Ben Hawkes
Flash Gordon
Category Self Promotion
Medium Collage
Brief A fun look at the fantastical
world of Flash Gordon whilst
adding my own take to the 1930's
comic book aesthetic.

Bish
On The Road
Category Self Promotion
Medium Digital and mixed media
Brief Produced whilst travelling on the road
in America. Here the lone cowboy enters
town after days alone and is faced with the
overload of signs and advertising.

Leighton Johns
Jake Fast - Kid Crusader
Category Self Promotion
Medium Digital
Brief Exploration of the visual language of vintage
'pulps' with a fictional 'Boy's Own' style book cover.

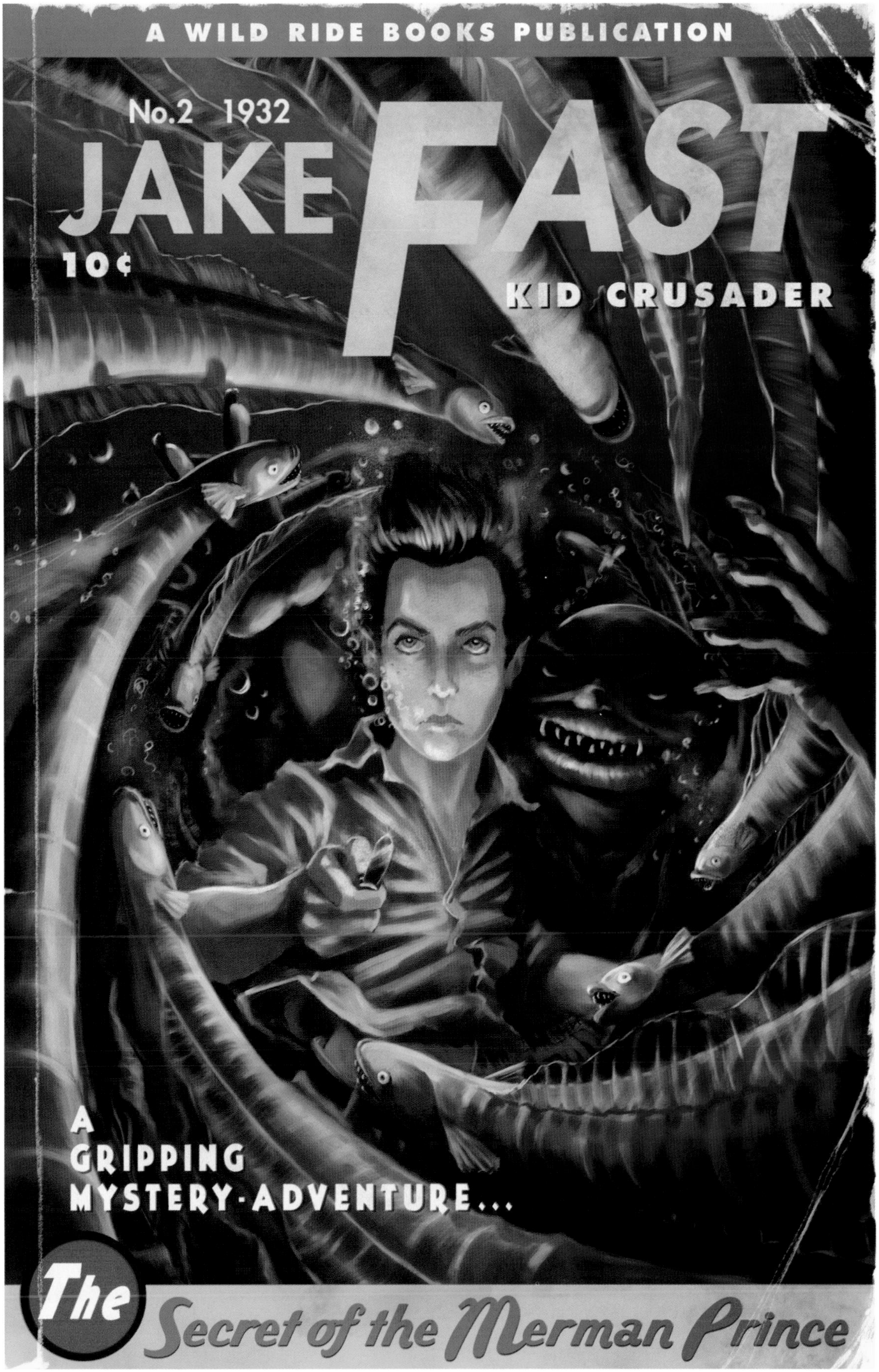

A WILD RIDE BOOKS PUBLICATION

No.2 1932

JAKE FAST

10¢

KID CRUSADER

A GRIPPING MYSTERY-ADVENTURE...

The Secret of the Merman Prince

Mark Oliver
Night Of The Wolf People
Category Self Promotion
Medium Screenprint
Brief Produced for the band Wolf People, in
response to the band name and it's relationship
to their music and identity as a group.

Katie May
Parisian Adventure
Category Self Promotion
Medium Ink, watercolour and digital
Brief Children's book spread, showing, with a
nostalgic feel, a little girl hurrying through the
hustle and bustle of a wintry Paris at twilight.

Cristina Guitian
Savanna Relaunch
Category Advertising
Medium Ink
Brief The Savanna Relaunch campaign gently
mocks London's archetypal subcultures. Cristina
was approached for her powers of surreal invention
and then given total freedom to create. The end
result is a series of unique characters and their pets
that have come to define the edginess of the brand.
Commissioned by Draftfcb London
Client Draftfcb London

Jerry Hoare
You Can't Teach An Old Dog New Tricks
Category Self Promotion
Medium Scraperboard and mixed media
Brief One of over 25 similar sized images
for a speculative publishing project: A luxury
illustrated book of proverbs and idioms.

Claudia Boldt
Star Gazers, Skyscrapers & Extraordinary Sausages
Category Children's Books
Medium Digital and mixed media
Brief Concept, text and illustration for a 32-page picture
book. The story tells about the friendship of the little girl,
called Henrietta and Frank, the dog.
Commissioned by Neil Burden
Client Child's Play (International)

Darren Diss
Spout
Category Editorial
Medium Mixed media
Brief Right wing Republicans tweeting and blogging about Obama not being American, claiming he was born in Kenya and not USA.
Commissioned by Kevin Bayliss
Client The Independent

Target
Category Editorial
Medium Mixed media
Brief Negative media comments relating to female politicians (Hazel Blears, Harriet Harman, Hillary Clinton) is driven by misogyny.
Commissioned by Kevin Bayliss
Client The Independent

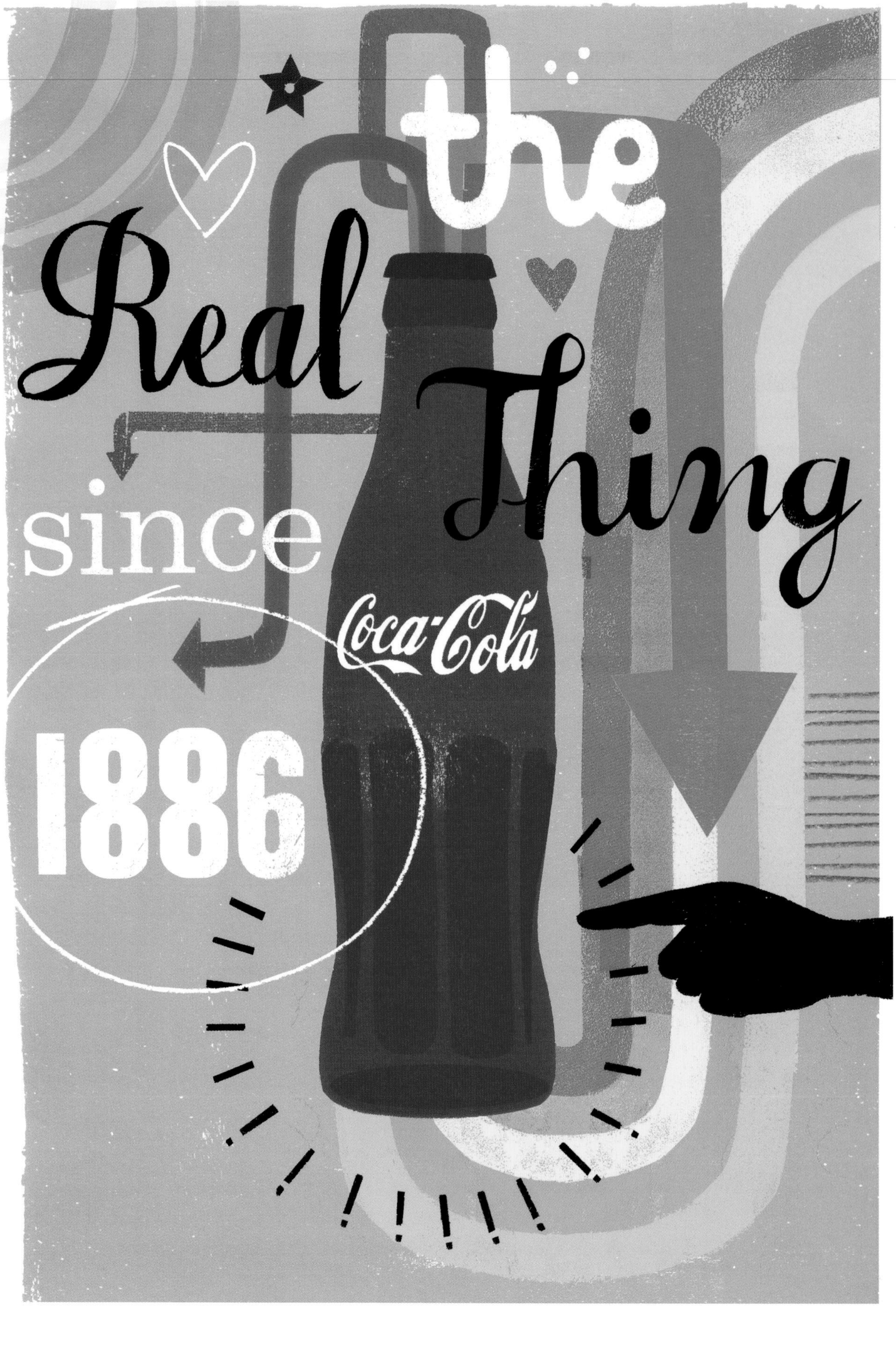

the
Real
Thing
since
1886
Coca-Cola

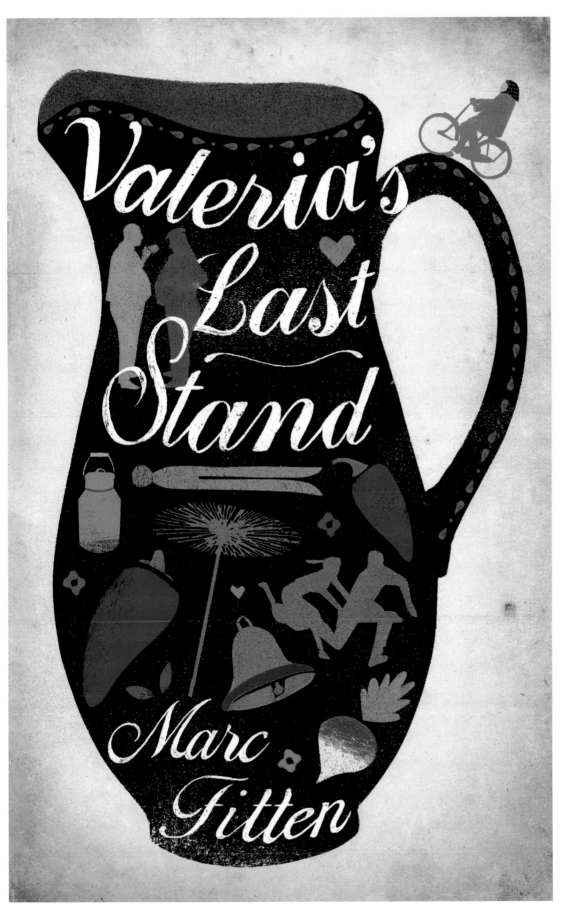

Jessie Ford
The Real Thing
Category Self Promotion
Medium Digital and mixed media
Brief To create a mock-up poster campaign for Coca-Cola.

Valeria's Last Stand
Category Books
Medium Digital and mixed media
Brief To create a cover for Bloomsbury Publishing that incorporated the title of the book within the image, and included symbols that feature in the story.
Commissioned by Sarah Morris
Client Bloomsbury

GMJ

Future London
Category Editorial
Medium Digital
Brief Wired UK wanted a high impact cover story to
mark their re-launch and set their editorial agenda.
We designed and created the cover that shows London
moving into the future. The backdrop photograph is by
Jason Hawkes.
Commissioned by Steve Peck
Client Conde Nast
Commissioned for WIRED UK May 09 re-launch issue

Piccadilly Circus – Peace And Power
Category Self Promotion
Medium Digital
Brief London's busiest thoroughfare is a haven of calm.
Sinking areas of land around the globe push rising
water levels ever higher. Lilies and fish now thrive in city
centres given over to energy generation.

Flooded London
Category Self Promotion
Medium Digital
Brief London, the new Venice. But where the city of the
gondola accommodates the water it sits in, London
has become uninhabitable, as every year the Thames
Barrier is overwhelmed by spring tides.

Mind Manager
Category Self Promotion
Medium Digital
Brief Medical science unlocks the secrets of the human
brain and nervous system. The latest must-have pocket
sized device will monitor your state of mind.

Simon Prescott
Small Mouse Big City
Category Children's Books
Medium Pencil and Watercolour
Brief Full colour artwork and cover for
a 32 page children's picture book.
Commissioned by Jude Evans
Client Little Tiger Press

Emily Milne Wallis
Mad Cow
Category Self Promotion
Medium Pen and Ink
Brief Exam project for BA (Hons) Illustration at
the University of Brighton. Original bought by the
University for the Michael Aldrich Collection.

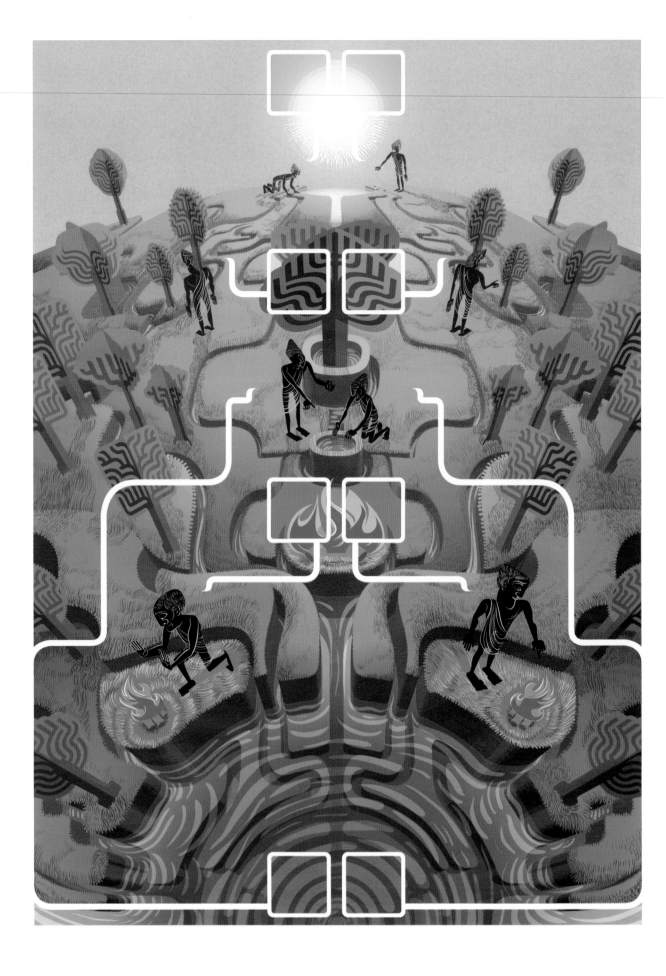

John Miers
Genesis 11:1
Category Self Promotion
Medium Digital
Brief "And the whole earth was of one language, and of one speech."

Genesis 11:7
Category Self Promotion
Medium Digital
Brief "Go to, let us go down, and there confound their language, that they may not understand one another's speech."

Ian Pollock
Rat
Category Editorial
Medium Ink
Brief Feature "Rodent Island".
Commissioned by Gary Cochran
Client Daily Telegraph Magazine

Duck With Fez On Scooter
Category Self Promotion
Medium Watercolour
Brief Drawing of Duck wearing
a Fez on a scooter.

TimeOut

London

LONDON'S WEEKLY LISTINGS BIBLE
WWW.TIMEOUT.COM/LONDON
MARCH 5 – 11 No.1959 £2.95

Hottest up and coming areas
The capital neighbourhoods you *can* afford to live in

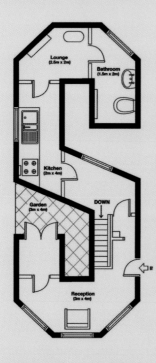
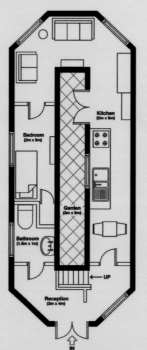
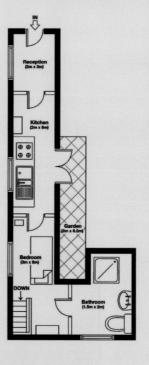
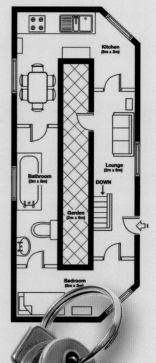

THE STRESS-FREE GUIDE TO HOME BUYING IN THE CAPITAL

From finding the perfect place to paying the right price, the ultimate contacts book for London house hunters

PLUS 'What are those whips for?' Doris Lessing exclusive interview

<

Tobatron
Sold
Category Editorial
Medium Digital
Brief Illustrate the word 'SOLD' in such a way
that it relates to the theme of house hunting.
Commissioned by Nick Booth
Client Time Out Magazine

Sam Gilbey
Flight Of The Conchords
Category Self Promotion
Medium Hand-drawn with a Wacom in Painter
and Photoshop
Brief I've always enjoyed doing portraits, and it's
a key component to my work, so paying tribute to
one of my favourite TV shows seemed like a great
idea for self promotion.

Graeme Neil Reid
Expedition To The Pole
Category Books
Medium Ink
Brief To supply illustration and design layout for
the chapter 'Scott of the Antarctic'.
Commissioned by Clare Hey
Client HarperCollins
Commissioned for The Dangerous Book of Heroes

Lawrence Of Arabia
Category Books
Medium Ink
Brief To supply illustration and design layout for
the chapter 'Lawrence of Arabia'.
Commissioned by Clare Hey
Client HarperCollins
Commissioned for The Dangerous Book of Heroes

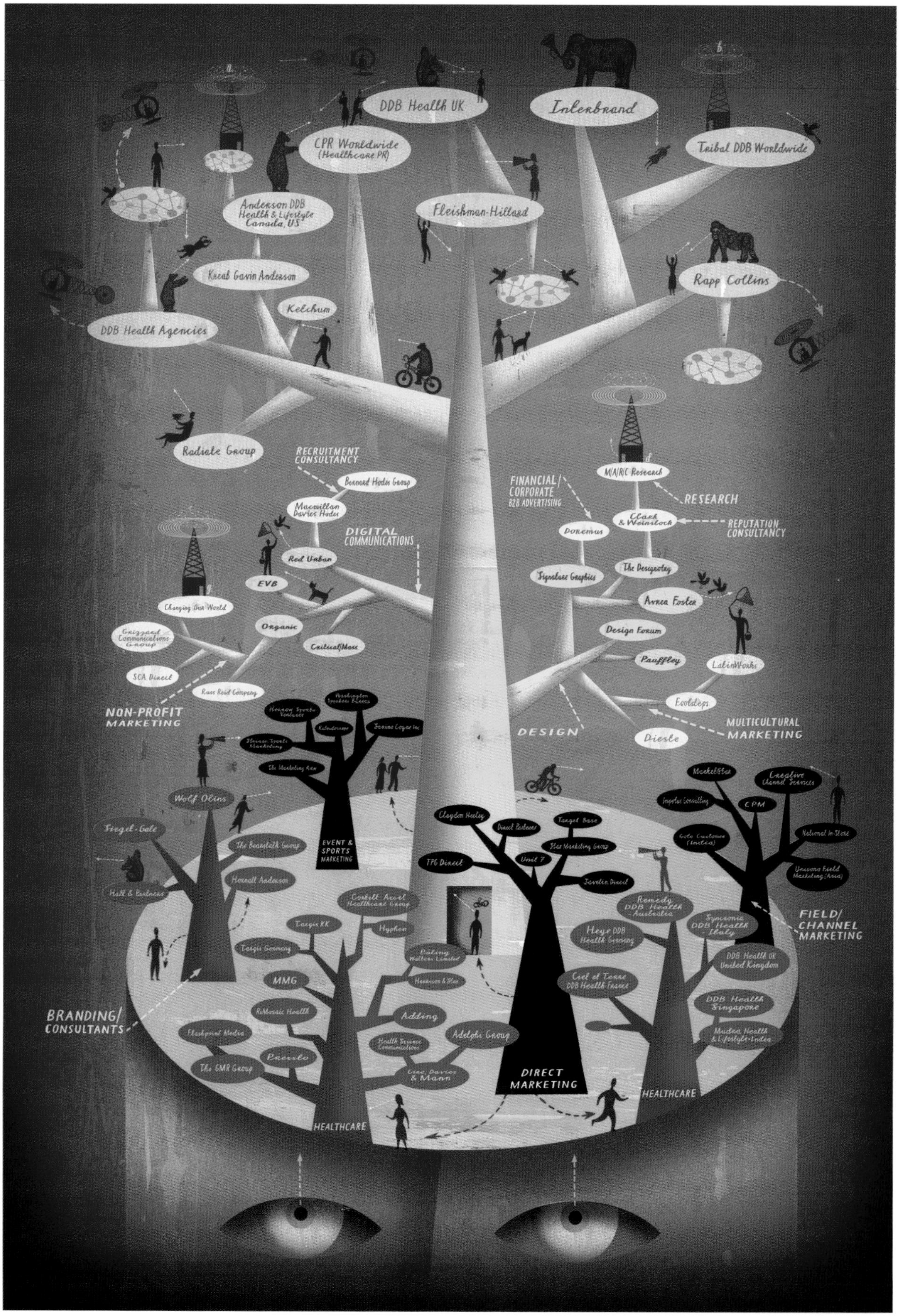

DDB Health UK
Interbrand
Tribal DDB Worldwide
CPR Worldwide (Healthcare PR)
Anderson DDB Health & Lifestyle Canada, US
Fleishman-Hillard
Kreab Gavin Anderson
Ketchum
Rapp Collins
DDB Health Agencies
Radiate Group
RECRUITMENT CONSULTANCY
Bernard Hodes Group
Macmillan Davies Hodes
DIGITAL COMMUNICATIONS
Red Urban
EVB
Changing Our World
Organic
CriticalMass
SCA Direct
Russ Reid Company
NON-PROFIT MARKETING
FINANCIAL/ CORPORATE B2B ADVERTISING
M/A/R/C Research
RESEARCH
Clark & Weinstock
REPUTATION CONSULTANCY
Doremus
Signature Graphics
The Designory
Arnell Foster
Design Forum
Pauffley
LatinWorks
Footsteps
DESIGN
MULTICULTURAL MARKETING
Washington Speakers Bureau
Kaleidoscope
The Marketing Arm
EVENT & SPORTS MARKETING
Wolf Olins
Siegel+Gale
The Beanstalk Group
Hornall Anderson
Hall & Partners
BRANDING/ CONSULTANTS
Corbett Accel Healthcare Group
Targis KK
Hyphen
Targis Germany
Paling Walters Limited
Harrison & Star
MMG
ReMosaic Health
Adding
Flashpoint Media
Health Science Communications
Adelphi Group
The GMR Group
Pressto
Cline, Davies & Mann
HEALTHCARE
Claydon Heeley
Direct Partners
Target Base
TPG Direct
Unit 7
Javelin Direct
DIRECT MARKETING
MarketStar
Creative Channel Services
Impulse Consulting
CPM
National In-Store
Remedy DDB Health - Australia
Syneonic DDB Health - Italy
Heye DDB Health Germany
DDB Health UK United Kingdom
Ciel et Terre DDB Health France
DDB Health Singapore
Mudra Health & Lifestyle-India
FIELD/ CHANNEL MARKETING
HEALTHCARE

Russell Cobb
DDB Forest
Category Advertising
Medium Digital and mixed media
Brief To visually show DBB's broad
and comprehensive expertise
through its affiliated companies.
Commissioned by Pete Mould
Client DDB

What To Do With This Card
Category Self Promotion
Medium Digital and mixed media
Brief Self promotion card. A playful card
playing on the idea of what to do with this
card (as opposed to throwing it away).

Sharon Tancredi
Taming The Savage Beast
Category Self Promotion
Medium Digital
Brief Personal work - no brief as such!

Tempest Rising
Category Books
Medium Digital
Brief Book cover for an urban fantasy novel about a
girl drawn into a dangerous and supernatural world.
Commissioned by Lauren Panepinto
Client Hachette Book Group
Commissioned for Orbit Books

Steve Simpson
Thinking Cat
Category Self Promotion
Medium Digital and mixed media
Brief Self-promotional portrait.

Aliens Stole My Underpants
Category Children's Books
Medium Digital
Brief Interior black & white illustrations for a poetry anthology by Brian Moses. Taking into consideration the poor quality paper, these had to be strong compositions and compliment the poems on the page.
Commissioned by Rachel Vale
Client Macmillan Children's Books

Chris Garbutt
Capsized Crunch
Category Self Promotion
Medium Digital
Brief Stretching the boundaries of the comic book form using mock cereal packaging and incorporating type.

Cereal Killers
Category Self Promotion
Medium Digital
Brief Stretching the boundaries of the comic book form using mock cereal packaging and incorporating type.

Alex T Smith
Egg
Category Children's Books
Medium Digital and mixed media
Brief A film noir style picture book featuring a Fox, an Egg, an Aligator and a troupe of dancing chickens. Nothing is as it seems...
Commissioned by Alison Still and Emma Layfield
Client Hodder Children's Books

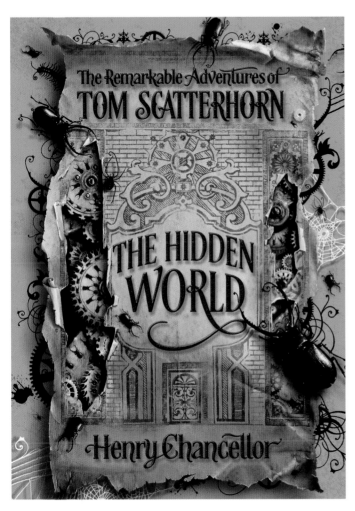

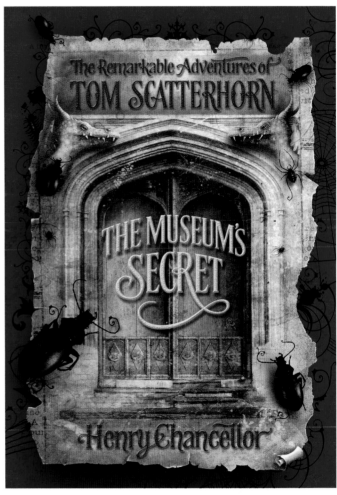

<

Jonny Duddle
The Pirate Cruncher
Category Children's Books
Medium Digital
Brief Captain Purplebeard and his crew of cut-throat pirates are off to find an island of treasure, but there's more to the island than it first appears. A story written and illustrated by Jonny Duddle.
Commissioned by Mike Jolley
Client Templar Publishing

Christopher Gibbs
The Hidden World
Category Books
Medium Digital and mixed media
Brief To produce a multi-layered image showing a drawn blueprint revealing the hidden mechanism created by the beetles inside, for the second book in the Remarkable Adventures of Tom Scatterhorn series.
Typography by Carol Kemp
Commissioned by Molly Dallas
Client Oxford University Press

The Museum's Secret
Category Books
Medium Digital and mixed media
Brief To produce a multi-layered image showing a parchment photo of the museum juxtaposed with the real insects to illustrate the different dimensions within the adventure story.
Typography by Carol Kemp
Commissioned by Molly Dallas
Client Oxford University Press

Tim Ellis
Bull Market For Electronics
Category Self Promotion
Medium Digital and mixed media
Brief To illustrate the idea of a bull
market for electronics.

Antoine Corbineau
Plus Is The New Minus
Category Self Promotion
Medium Digital and mixed media
Brief Climate change – it's time to lead.

Jonny Voss
City1
Category Self Promotion
Medium Ink
Brief Personal work from sketchbooks.

Melissa Launay
The Gathering
Category Design
Medium Acrylic
Brief An open interpretation for the
2009 Spring Festival of Cordoba,Spain.
Canvas size: 10 x 4.5 meters.
Commissioned by Vimcorsa
Client Vimcorsa
Commissioned for El Jardin de la Casa

Riding Gold Lion
Category Self Promotion
Medium Gouache
Brief A painting commissioned for Karen O of the
YEAH YEAH YEAHS. Karen O riding a bunny cat
dressed as a gold lion in a enchanted forest.

‹

Zara Picken
A View of London
Category Self Promotion
Medium Digital and mixed media
Brief To create an image celebrating the vibrancy of present-day London, reflecting aspects of the capital, which the illustrator relates to and enjoys and incorporating a transport element.

Robin Chevalier
Sold Out
Category Design
Medium Digital and mixed media
Brief To illustrate a theme of "Not enough fish in the sea" for a brochure produced by the Marine Conservation Society. Illustration supplied on a charitable basis.
Client Marine Conservation Society

Gail Armstrong
Henry VIII - Man And Monarch
Category Design
Medium 3D paper sculpture
Brief A set of stamps highlighting key
aspects of the reign of Henry VIII - his coronation,
his pastimes since youth, the sinking of The
Mary Rose, meeting Francis I at the Field of The
Cloth of Gold.
Commissioned by Dawn Gill
Client Guernsey Post Ltd
photography by Jonny Thompson

Environmental Globe
Category Design
Medium 3D paper sculpture
Brief To create an image for international
company PALL that positively reflects its
environmentally sound filtration and purification
solutions for a variety of industries.
Commissioned by Keith Groshans
Client Curran & Connors, Inc.
Commissioned for PALL Corporation
photography by Jonny Thompson

Barbara Vagnozzi
Rosetta And Dragon
Category Self Promotion
Medium Acrylic
Brief Project for a children's book.

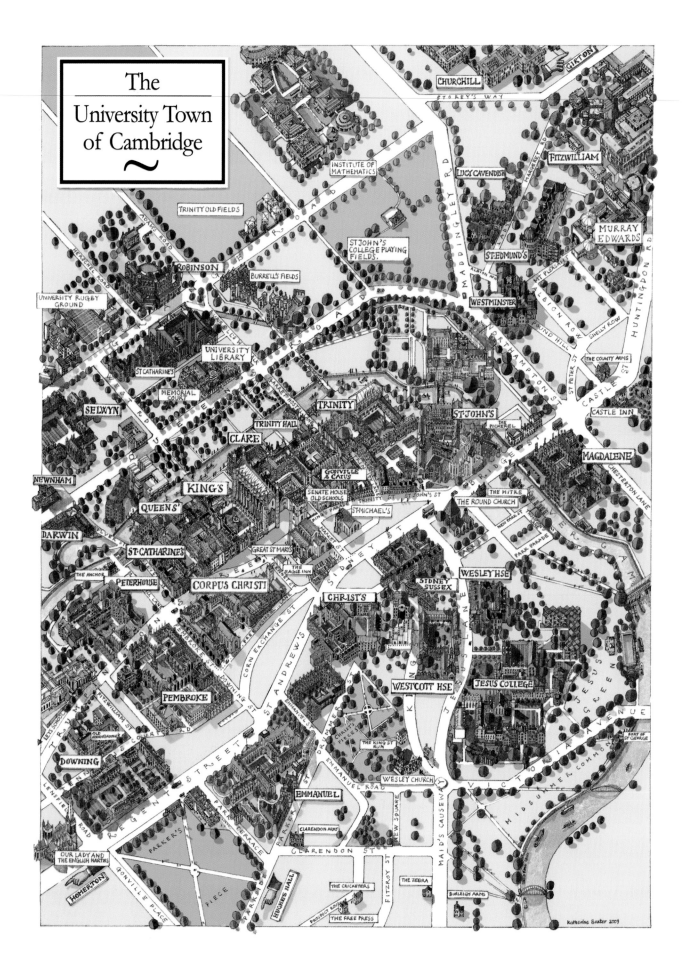

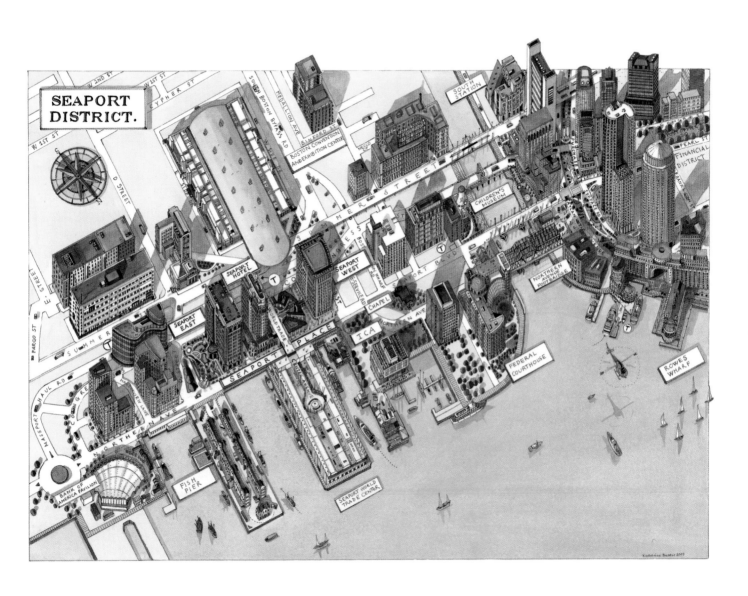

Katherine Baxter
Cambridge
Category Advertising
Medium Watercolour
Brief To illustrate an aerial map of Central
Cambridge containing the Colleges of The
University of Cambridge, to be advertised in
the Cambridge Alumni Magazine.
Commissioned by Nick Dawe
Client Folio Boutique

Boston Seaport
Category Advertising
Medium Watercolour
Brief Produce an artist's bird's eye view of
Boston Seaport area, making the hotel and
exhibition center the focal point.
Commissioned by Michael Panagako
Client Brand and Beyond
Commissioned for Seaport Place (Hotel)

Wesley's Britain
Category Advertising
Medium Digital and mixed media
Brief To show the life and travels of John
Wesley, the founder of the Methodist Church.
Commissioned by
Rev, the Lord Griffiths of Burry Port
Client Wesley's Chapel
Commissioned for Methodist Church

WESLEY'S CHAPEL
Built in 1778 on the site of the Old Foundary. John Wesley preached, lived and died here. He is buried in a tomb behind the Chapel. Site of 'The Museum of Methodism' and an active Congregation.

EPWORTH RECTORY
Samuel Wesley was Rector here from 1697-1735 and lies buried in the Churchyard. And his sons John (1703) and Charles (1707) were born here. They escaped a devastating fire in 1709.

ENGLESEA BROOK
Museum of Primitive Methodism is in a Chapel opened in 1832 and associated with William Clowes and Hugh Bourne. The first Camp meetings were held on nearby Mow Cop in 1807 and some meetings lasted over 14 hours

THE NEW ROOM BRISTOL
The first Preaching House built by John Wesley in 1739, the Oldest Methodist building in the World. Charles Wesley lived here, after his marriage he lived in nearby Charles Street.

THE ALDERSGATE FLAME
On Aldersgate St. London, stands a bronze memorial flame commemorating John Wesley's conversion experience on this site on May 24 1738. He described his conversion in his journal "I felt my heart strangely warmed"

Eleftheria Alexandri
Snakes And Ladders
Category Self Promotion
Medium Digital
Brief A reflection of my experiences as I took
my first steps towards achieving professional
recognition as an illustrator.

Ostrich
Category Self Promotion
Medium Digital
Brief An imaginative interpretation of the 'ostrich',
both the animal and the person who tries to
escape their current situation.

<

Bisi Wakeham
Kussnacht Am Rigi
Category Self Promotion
Medium Digital
Brief A personal project based on my
experience of a first trip to Switzerland.

Tim Laing
...She Now Obeyed The OD Youth.
She Crouched In Under The Stairs
Category Books
Medium Pencil
Brief To read the book and select nine scenes to
illustrate, supplying full page black and white for
the Folio Society edition of 'Schindler's Ark'.
Commissioned by Sheri Gee
Client The Folio Society

Anna Bhushan
Aziz Stood At The Window Inhaling The City
Category Books
Medium Watercolour and gouache
Brief To read the book and select nine scenes to
illustrate, supplying full page colour for the Folio
Society edition of 'Midnight's Children'.
Commissioned by Eleanor Crow
Client The Folio Society

James Fryer
Planet Overload
Category Editorial
Medium Acrylic
Brief The world will not be able to cope with the predicted population growth.
Commissioned by David Gibbons
Client New Statesman magazine

Gloomy Outlook
Category Editorial
Medium Acrylic
Brief Chinese factory closures. There's a gloomy outlook for China as the economic downturn causes many factories to close.
Commissioned by Adrian Taylor
Commissioned for CPO Agenda magazine

Firm But Fair
Category Editorial
Medium Acrylic
Brief To show how you can be firm with your clients but still maintain good customer relations.
Commissioned by Adrian Taylor
Commissioned for CPO Agenda magazine

Watchdog?
Category Editorial
Medium Acrylic
Brief To show a regulatory body (watchdog) whose bark is far worse than its bite. A watchdog that ducks the most troublesome issues.
Commissioned by Chris Barber
Client Times Higher Education magazine

<

Kate Slater
Find The Golden Egg
Category Advertising
Medium Collage
Brief One of three posters commissioned to
promote Ethel's Chocolate Lounge and their
Easter competition.
Commissioned by Carlie Naftolin
Client Zig
Commissioned for Ethel's Chocolate Lounge

Jill Latter
Gilbert Was Very Cross
Category Children's Books
Medium Watercolour and ink
Brief This is one of the illustrations for the story,
Gilbert's Boat, which was accepted at the Bologna
Book Fair March 09 by North South Books.
Commissioned by Frances McKay
Client Nord- Sud Books, (North South Books)

Tim Stevens
The Flying King
Category Self Promotion
Medium Watercolour
Brief There was once a Devil who liked to eat small children. 'How would you like to fly?' asked the Devil. 'Very much indeed' said the King, 'but what do you want in return?' - by Terry Jones.

Howl's Moving Castle
Category Self Promotion
Medium Watercolour
Brief 'They seized a velvet cloak each and flung them on. Sophie got one that turned it's wearer into a red-bearded man. In the other one Michael was a horse.' - by Dianna Wynne Jones.

Paul Cox
Flatiron
Category Self Promotion
Medium Watercolour
Brief To do a painting of this exceptional triangular building on a junction of Broadway in New York, by emphasising its impact on the street landscape.

Palio
Category Self Promotion
Medium Watercolour
Brief To capture the excitement of this horse race around the historic campo of Siena.

Carlton Hotel
Category Self Promotion
Medium Watercolour
Brief To paint an atmospheric image of the Carlton Hotel in Cannes.

Hartwig Braun
Zero Degrees Longitude (Greenwich)
Category Self Promotion
Medium Outlines drawn by hand and coloured digitally
Brief Drawn freehand to show the Greenwich area in my quirky, yet very detailed, fish-eye perspective.

Jane Anderson
Laurie
Category Self Promotion
Medium Digital
Brief Commission for an illustrative portrait.

Chris Vine
Food Map Of Spain
Category Editorial
Medium ink and watercolour
Brief A map of Spain showing regional food and drink. This image supported a series of articles describing Spanish culinary history.
Commissioned by Roger Standen
Client Design Dimension
Commissioned for Cook School Magazine

The Silver Spoon for Children

Favourite Italian Recipes

Harriet Russell
The Silver Spoon For Children
Category Books
Medium Digital and mixed media
Brief Cover for Italian cookery book, aimed
at children aged 10 - 14.
Commissioned by Amanda Renshaw
Client Phaidon Press

Mount Fuji
Category Design
Medium Digital and mixed media
Brief Designs for a set of travel stickers featuring
Radley the dog travelling to different destinations.
Commissioned by Natalie Bolton
Client Radley

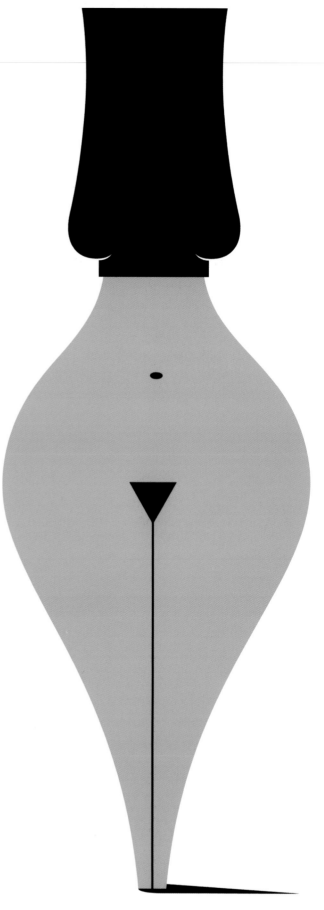

Joe McLaren
Oscars 2009
Category Editorial
Medium Digital and mixed media
Brief An Oscars special focusing on how
the Brits conquered this year's Oscars.
Commissioned by Alex Breuer
Client The Times
Commissioned for Times2

Noma Bar
Female Erotic Writing
Category Editorial
Medium Digital
Brief To illustrate how women are just as
good at writing about sex as men.
Commissioned by Emma Woodroofe
Client The Times
Commissioned for Saturday Review

Nathalie Lees
A Novel Approach To Cooking
Category Editorial
Medium Digital and mixed media
Brief To illustrate a piece about cooking
recipes that appear in literature.
Commissioned by Emma Woodroofe
Client The Times
Commissioned for Weekend

Tobias Hickey
Dilemma
Category Editorial
Medium Digital and mixed media
Brief To illustrate the question about the eternal
parental dilemma, "How can we teach our
teenage children to have a healthy attitude to sex,
but prevent them from actually having any?".
Commissioned by Martin Harrison
Client The Times
Commissioned for Weekend

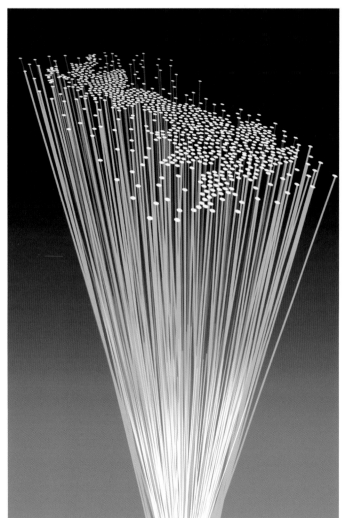

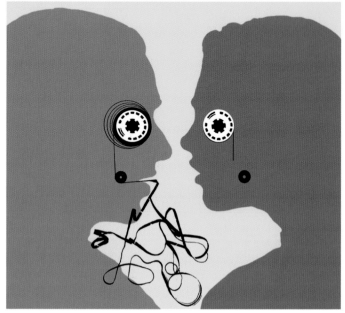

›

Tobias Hickey
Broadband Britain
Category Editorial
Medium Digital and mixed media
Brief Government plans for broadband access.
Commissioned by John-Henry Barac
Client The Guardian G2

Falling On Deaf Ears
Category Editorial
Medium Mixed media
Brief My girlfriend of seven years doesn't listen to me.
Commissioned by Martin Harrison
Client The Times
Commissioned for Weekend - Body And Soul

James De La Rue
King D'Tong's Palace
Category Children's Books
Medium Ink
Brief Interior illustration for David Grimstone's "Gladiator Boy" series.
Commissioned by Leilani Sparrow
Client Hodder Children's Books

Jemma Robinson
Manhattan
Category Self Promotion
Medium Digital and mixed media
Brief Image response to: "Close atmosphere today. Need the rain to breakthrough. Heady, clammy, intense air. Storm on in." Part of the self initiated project 'We Have A Nice Day'.

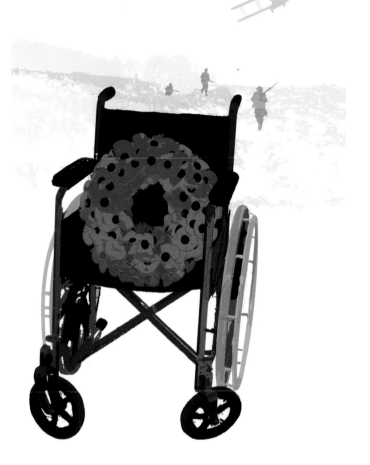

P.D.A
Category Self Promotion
Medium Digital and mixed media
Brief Image response to statement "My life is a public spectacle. Enjoy the show. I'll be here all week." Part of the self-initiated "We Have A Nice Day" project with writer Michelle Bower .

Harry Patch
Category Editorial
Medium Digital and mixed media
Brief Image about the death of the last WWI veteran Harry Patch. Headline: "We have every reason to grieve for Harry Patch and his time".
Commissioned by Dan Barber
Client The Independent

Ceri Patmore
To Do List
Category Self Promotion
Medium Collage, Stencil, Airbrushed Acrylic
Brief An image depicting when life's necessary chores become overwhelming.

Robin Boyden
A Name But No Horse
Category Self Promotion
Medium Digital
Brief An illustration supporting the late Clement Freud's love of horse racing.

Scotophobia
Category Self Promotion
Medium Digital
Brief An illustration communicating Scotophobia - the fear of the dark.

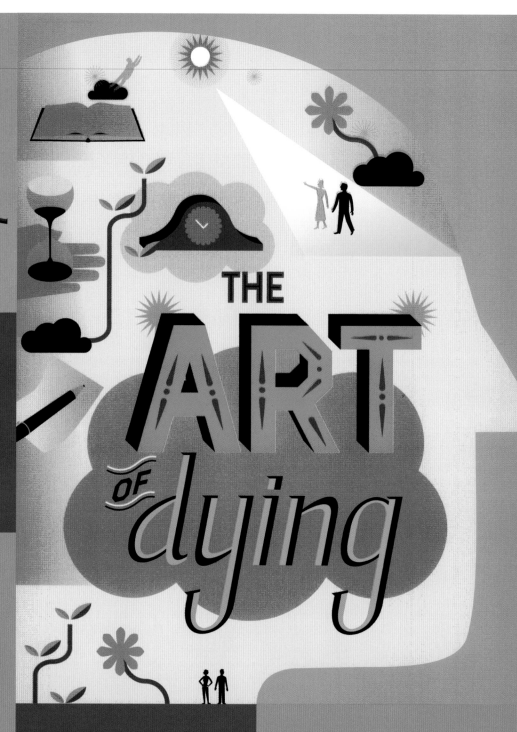

THE ART OF dying

PETER FENWICK ELIZABETH FENWICK

continuum

Andrew Baker
The Art of Dying
Category Books
Medium Digital and mixed media
Brief To design, Illustrate and letter the
cover to convey the content without
dwelling on its darker aspects.
Commissioned by Nick Evans
Client Continuum Books

The Father Paoli Baldi Mysteries
Category Design
Medium Digital and mixed media
Brief For use on a CD for the BBC's Radio Crimes
series of audio dramatisations, this image had
to convey the essence of the Father Paoli Baldi
Mysteries without portraying the protagonists.
Commissioned by Dick Evry
Client BBC Audio Books

I woke up
under the Snowtrees
in a cradle of roots. The branches
dripped sunlit water around my head.
I'd been told about this forest. "It attracts
the wrong crowd", I'd heard. I wasn't convinced.
I could hear wolves treading icy crackles somewhere almost
close, and cold crept in where my coat didn't meet my trousers.
But I didn't want to move. I was happy looking straight ahead at
the branches tickling the sharp blue morning. Snowtrees had perfect
fractal features at this time of year, and there wasn't long to wait before
they expired. Today or tomorrow they'd come apart all at once, in
whispering white-gold explosions. One tree becomes a thousand pale
fragments, making a soft, deep cover for the ground. The whole forest
bursts into a shimmering blizzard and then a freezing flatness. People
witnessing this feel a release, as with fireworks and demolitions, and great
distance is travelled to be within it. I was, by some forgotten accident,
in a prime position, if only it would happen before I got too cold.
Sniffing and howling from the wolves now, and I thought about
the tension my absence might be causing at home. They weren't
expecting me at any particular time, and the moon seemed to say
I wasn't worryingly late, yet. I could hear others arriving
to watch. "Any minute now, someday soon"
we said, and wondered why anyone
wouldn't want to be here.
Cosying into the frost
and the crunch,
all we had to do
was wait.

Sarah J. Coleman
Snowtrees
Category Self Promotion
Medium Ink
Brief I commissioned my friend, writer Ed Garland,
to write me a piece for the winter season, supplying
him with only a handful of key words. The resulting
piece I illustrated for my seasonal mailout.

Happy Birthday Housing Works
Category Design
Medium Ink and Digital
Brief Celebrating the first birthday of the Housing
Works online shop, which services the housing
and health needs of people with AIDS by selling
pre-owned designer clothing and vintage items.
Commissioned by Diana Boric
Client Housing Works

Kevin Hauff
Mojo Man
Category Self Promotion
Medium Digital and mixed media
Brief Mojo Man: Image exploring a delusional
middle age man's self perception when
undergoing a mid life crisis.

Eco Flight
Category Self Promotion
Medium Digital and mixed media
Brief Image exploring the potential for airline
companies to invest in research for ecologically
responsible alternatives to traditional air travel.

Economic Burn Out
Category Self Promotion
Medium Digital and mixed media
Brief Image exploring the sudden burn
out of the global economy.

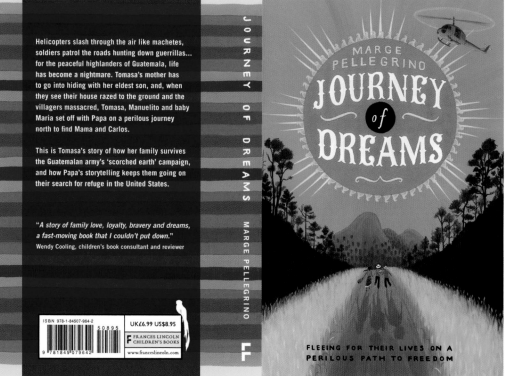

David Dean
The Elephant's Tale
Category Children's Books
Medium Acrylic
Brief This is the fourth in a series, so had to be in keeping with the earlier covers but also have it's own character. The book is an adventure story set in the Namibian desert.
Commissioned by Jane Hughes
Client Orion Children's Books

Journey Of Dreams
Category Children's Books
Medium Acrylic
Brief The brief was for a cover that looked "exciting, dramatic and edgy, with a colour palette to match! Perhaps incorporating Guatemalan embroidery elements".
Commissioned by Jane Donald
Client Frances Lincoln Children's Books

Rachel Gannon
South
Category Self Promotion
Medium Mixed media
Brief Self initiated work. Ideas for a children's book to promote my illustration in this area. A bird who has to find his own way south for the winter, when he is accidentally left behind.

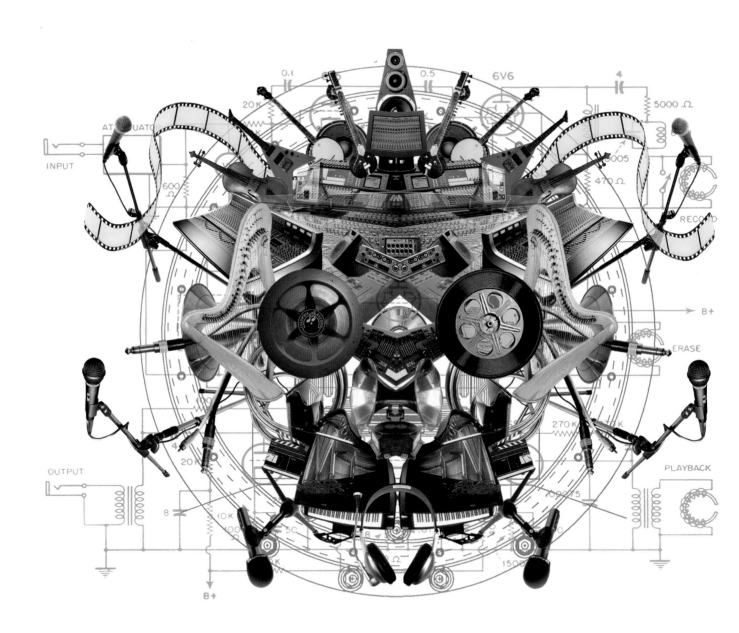

Miles Cole
Audiobug
Category Advertising
Medium Digital
Brief Create an iconic image for music
supervisors Foundtracks, an organic
creature comprised of audiovisual imagery.
Commissioned by Glenn Marshall
Client Foundtracks

Tesco Invasion High St
Category Editorial
Medium Digital and mixed media
Brief Create an imposing image of Tesco as a
malign force taking over Britain's high streets.
Commissioned by Clayton Crabtree
Client Newsquest Media
Commissioned for Insurance Times

Jonathan Lam
Stray
Category Self Promotion
Medium Digital and mixed media
Brief The image was used in an exhibition I did with a group of graduates from Middlesex University. The idea was to depict someone who was lost in the big city, a feeling reflected by a lot of graduates.

Jonathan Lam and Annie Dalton
Category Self Promotion
Medium Digital and mixed media
Brief To create an image to help promote an art exhibition held in Brick Lane. The image was used as a poster at Moorgate tube station, leaflets, website etc.

Simon Spilsbury
Opera
Category Editorial
Medium Ink
Brief 1 of 6 pieces used to illustrate New Year hobbies.
Commissioned by Richard Keenan
Client Time Out Magazine

John Holcroft
Taking Their Fill
Category Self Promotion
Medium Digital and mixed media
Brief About chief bankers earning fat bonuses and hefty pensions during the economic downturn.

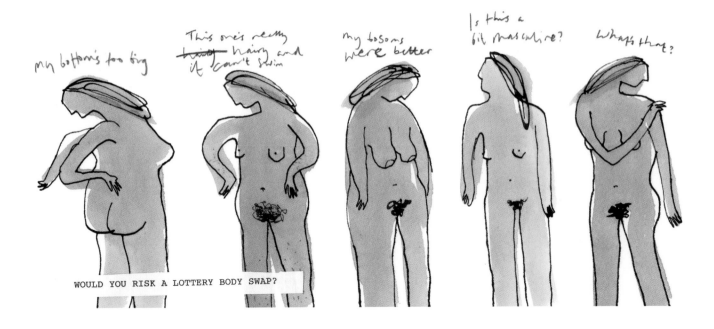

Simon Brader
Hops
Category Editorial
Medium Digital and mixed media
Brief Full page Illustration to accompany an article
on how the selection of hops and their oils are
essential to the distinctive flavour of a beer.
Commissioned by Sally Toms
Client Paragraph Publishing Ltd
Commissioned for Beers of the World

Anna Steinberg
Body Lottery
Category Self Promotion
Medium Ink
Brief Self initiated project inspired by a
normal shaped and attractive woman
who obsessed about her body.

Climate Change People
Category New Media
Medium Ink
Brief Simple, accessible, contemporary characters,
to be shown alongside responses to issues of
climate change. E.g: 'I recycle, I've changed my
light bulbs, I buy organic fruit. I've done my bit.'
Commissioned by Steve Colling
Client Onearth

Tony Healey
Cristiano Ronaldo
Category Editorial
Medium Pencil and digital
Brief Caricature portrait of former Manchester
United footballer Cristiano Ronaldo, used to
accompany a profile article.
Commissioned by Wayne Caba
Client The Daily Telegraph

Mark Hughes
Category Editorial
Medium Pencil and digital
Brief Supply a caricature portrait of Manchester
City manager Mark Hughes, to accompany a
profile article.
Commissioned by Wayne Caba
Client The Daily Telegraph

Fabio Capello
Category Editorial
Medium Pencil and digital
Brief Supply a caricature portrait of
England football manager Fabio Capello,
to accompany a profile article.
Commissioned by Wayne Caba
Client The Daily Telegraph

Al Pacino
Category Editorial
Medium Pencil and digital
Brief Supply 1/4 page colour caricature
portrait of Al Pacino in character to
accompany a magazine article.
Commissioned by Anna Goodson
Client AGM
Commissioned for Reader's Digest

Cathy Fisher
Contain
Category Self Promotion
Medium Mixed media
Brief Illustrate an image of
a caged bird for a children's
book about dreams.

Yvonne Lee
Good Times Gone
Category Self Promotion
Medium Digital and mixed media
Brief Self set brief based on a story
of love destroyed by a life of card
gambling and drugs.

**Confidentiality And Children
With HIV**
Category Editorial
Medium Digital and mixed media
Brief Illustrate article about the
importance of confidentiality when
treating HIV positive children to
prevent them being stigmatised.
Commissioned by Minesh Parmar
Client RCN Publishing Co
Commissioned for Paediatric Nursing

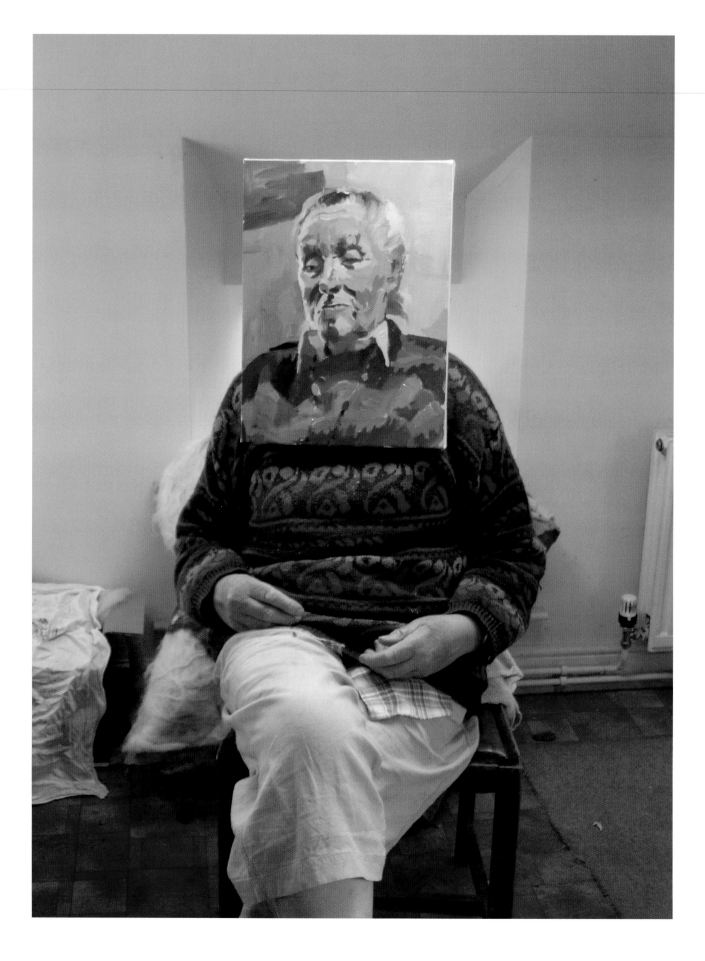

Andrew Bylo
Customised Mother-in-law
Category Editorial
Medium Photo of painting in context
Brief Submit work that features customising
to accompany feature on the artist.
Commissioned by Richard Brereton
Client Magma Books
Commissioned for Graphic Magazine

Katharine McEwen
Bruno
Category Self Promotion
Medium Collage
Brief This is the first page from an unpublished
children's book I have written called "Bruno"
about the antics of a bear as he prepares to
hibernate for the winter.

Zebedee's Zoo
Category Children's Books
Medium Gouache, watercolour and pencil crayon
Brief The zoo animals in this story party all night,
which explains their laziness during the day. This
final page reads, "So children, if you want to visit
the zoo, go there at night from 10 until 2!".
Commissioned by Kate Burns
Client Orchard Books
Commissioned for 'Zebedee's Zoo' by Giles Milton

Osmand Nosse
Everything's Grand
Category Self Promotion
Medium Digital and mixed media
Brief From the daily blog acatisacat.blogspot.com:
I like: owls, words like 'yachts', skiffle music, marmalade
and when dogs yawn and sound like they are saying
something. I once heard a terrier yawn the name 'Philip',
seriously... he said 'Philip'.

Allan Sanders
Secret Agent Man
Category Self Promotion
Medium Digital and mixed media
Brief A piece of personal work exploring
the world of international espionage.

Glen McBeth
Half Crown Nation
Category Editorial
Medium Digital and mixed media
Brief To illustrate how King William IV was eager
not to look like he was spending too much money
on his Coronation of 1831. In difficult economic
times he didn't want to look too ostentatious.
Commissioned by Susanne Frank
Client BBC History Magazine

Bill Butcher
The Monza Grand Prix
Category Editorial
Medium Digital
Brief To illustrate the fact that the modern Monza Grand Prix is still steeped in the tradition and spirit of the early races of the forties and fifties.
Commissioned by Ben Turner
Client Financial Times
Commissioned for
How To Spend It

The Potential Of A Clean-tech Partnership
Category Editorial
Medium Digital
Brief Only collaboration between China and the US will create an environment where clean-energy technology will thrive.
Commissioned by Delilah Zak
Client Mckinsey Quarterly website

Dean Beattie
The Underground
Category Self Promotion
Medium Mixed media
Brief I wanted to create a crowded scene on the
London underground - which invited the viewer's
eye to wander around and take in all the detail.

Accident And Emergency
Category Self Promotion
Medium Mixed media
Brief In this image I wanted to create an Accident
& Emergency Room for broken toys. This was
based on an old brief which looked at the idea of
children throwing broken toys away - rather than
fixing them.

Monica Capoferri
The Birdwatcher
Category Books
Medium Ink
Brief To illustrate a chapter reflecting on being still and quiet, with all the senses tuned to what is around – like a bird watcher.
Commissioned by Alison Barr
Client SPCK Publishing
Commissioned for Mirror Images by David Adam

SEAN LEE

CARICATURIST ★

Steven Carroll
Caricaturist
Category Self Promotion
Medium Scraperboard
Brief Experimental caricature of
artist Sean Lee depicted in the style
of a Russian silent film poster.

Dave Arcari
Category Design
Medium Scraperboard
Brief To produce an illustration of slide guitarist
and songwriter Dave Arcari for his independent
record label that specialises in alternative roots
music with an insurgent twist.
Commissioned by Dave Arcari
Client Buzz Records

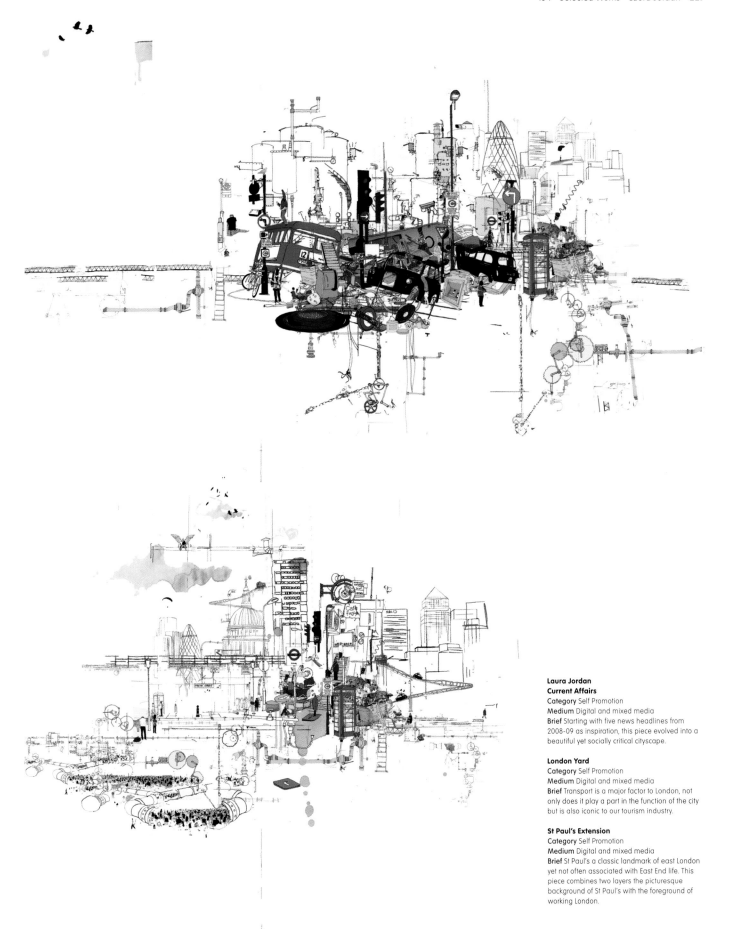

Laura Jordan
Current Affairs
Category Self Promotion
Medium Digital and mixed media
Brief Starting with five news headlines from
2008-09 as inspiration, this piece evolved into a
beautiful yet socially critical cityscape.

London Yard
Category Self Promotion
Medium Digital and mixed media
Brief Transport is a major factor to London, not
only does it play a part in the function of the city
but is also iconic to our tourism industry.

St Paul's Extension
Category Self Promotion
Medium Digital and mixed media
Brief St Paul's a classic landmark of east London
yet not often associated with East End life. This
piece combines two layers the picturesque
background of St Paul's with the foreground of
working London.

Daniel Pudles
Coffee Without The Grind
Category Editorial
Medium Woodcut and digital
Brief Book review illustration for Anthony
Capella's "The various flavours of coffee",
a gourmet and erotic fiction.
Commissioned by Suzy Connolly
Client The Economist Books and Arts section

Man, Machine And In-between
Category Editorial
Medium woodcut and digital
Brief An article on the new challenges of
the ethics of brain-implantable devices.
Commissioned by Barbara Izdebska
Client Nature Publishing Group
Commissioned for Nature Journal of Science

Ralph Steadman
Foot Sprite
Category Self Promotion
Medium Mixed media
Brief Promotional piece to
accompany talk in America.

Whyisbox
Dusty Frazzle
Category Self Promotion
Medium Digital
Brief Created as a self-promotional piece
for an article in NewSugar magazine.

Ian Whadcock
Should You Become A Banker To Your Key Suppliers?
Category Editorial
Medium Digital
Brief The article is about how CPOs can read the signs of cash distress in their suppliers and whether they should act as a banker to their suppliers during the the credit crunch/downturn.
Commissioned by Adrian Taylor
Client Redactive
Commissioned for CPO Agenda

Should I Have The Hots For A Heat Pump?
Category Editorial
Medium Digital
Brief Ground Source Heat Pumps – 'In my opinion heat-pump technology is overrated and oversold, tapping into consumers' fears over rising energy costs and their desires to be "green"'.
Commissioned by Catalina Sogden
Client The Sunday Telegraph: Living

Creative Ways To Survive The Downturn
Category Editorial
Medium Digital
Brief Changing shift patterns, reducing the working week, wage freezes, cuts in salary, flexible working hours, unpaid leave/sabbaticals - ways in which employers can save money on staff.
Commissioned by Dinah Lone
Client Haymarket Professional
Commissioned for Print Week

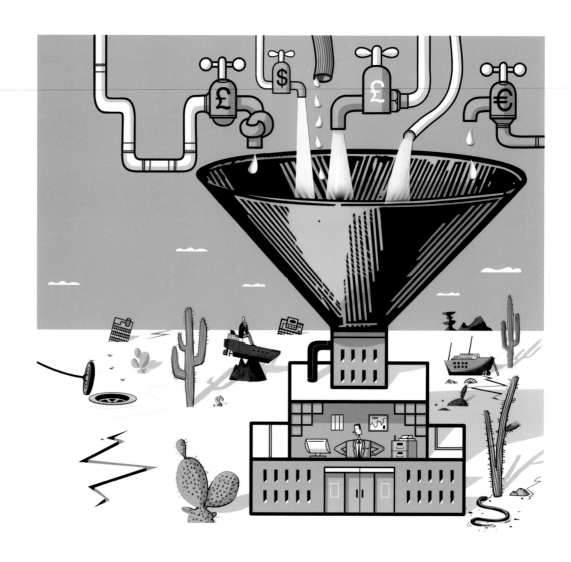

Ian Whadcock
King Cash
Category Editorial
Medium Digital
Brief Businesses don't go bust-they run out
of cash. In the "real recession" collecting cash
becomes the number one business priority.
It's important not to ignore any potential
source of funds.
Commissioned by John Poile
Client Institute of Directors
Commissioned for Director Magazine

Hair Length In Florida Theme Parks: An
Approximation of Hair Length In The USA
Category Editorial
Medium Digital
Brief Improbable Research Column: "To obtain
data on the percentage of persons in the
US with different lengths of scalp hair". Data
derived from theme park observations.
Commissioned by Alice Woolley
Client The Guardian: G2 Education

Gemma Latimer
Bird Talk
Category Design
Medium Digital and mixed media
Brief I Dress Myself presents "Birds" a T-shirt design competition. To create a design using the above subject.
Commissioned by Peter and Hannah Conway
Client I Dress Myself

Jonas Bergstrand
Collage Street
Category Self Promotion
Medium Collage
Brief Promotional poster sized print.
Distributed and sold via agent's website.

Over At Maradona's Place
Category Self Promotion
Medium Digital
Brief Caricature of Maradona. Additional faces
that appear in the image are Fidel Castro, Che
Guevara and footballer Juan Román Riquelme.

Jonathan Williams
BMX Bandit
Category Editorial
Medium Digital
Brief To illustrate a BMX bandit called Benjamin
- 43 year old design agency worker with 'gnarly'
attitude - for an article about biker tribes.
Commissioned by Emma Woodroofe
Client News International
Commissioned for The Times Weekend

Darwin 200
Category Editorial
Medium Digital
Brief Portrait of Charles Darwin as a young man
(c.1840) commissioned by Nature magazine to
celebrate the 200th anniversary of his birth.
Commissioned by Barbara Izdebska
Client Macmillan
Commissioned for Nature

Allan Deas
War
Category Design
Medium Digital and mixed media
Brief To come up with a 'visual cover version' for
the song WAR by Edwin Star.
Commissioned by Colm Larkin
Client Hidden Depths
Commissioned for 'It's Pop It's Art' by Airside

Sarah Hanson
The Danube: Tales Of The River Bank
Category Editorial
Medium Digital and mixed media
Brief The illustration should follow the footsteps
of the writer and include elements from his
travels, such as his chosen transport, landmarks
and landscapes he encounters along the way.
(4 page illustration).
Commissioned by Jamie McPherson
Client Cedar Communications

Stephen Fry: In America (Chapter 1)
Category Books
Medium Digital and mixed media
Brief Illustrate Stephen Fry's journey across
America in his black taxicab (for the chapter
openers). Each illustration should have a feel
that is unique to the places they represent,
with space for titles.
Commissioned by Faith Booker
Client HarperCollins

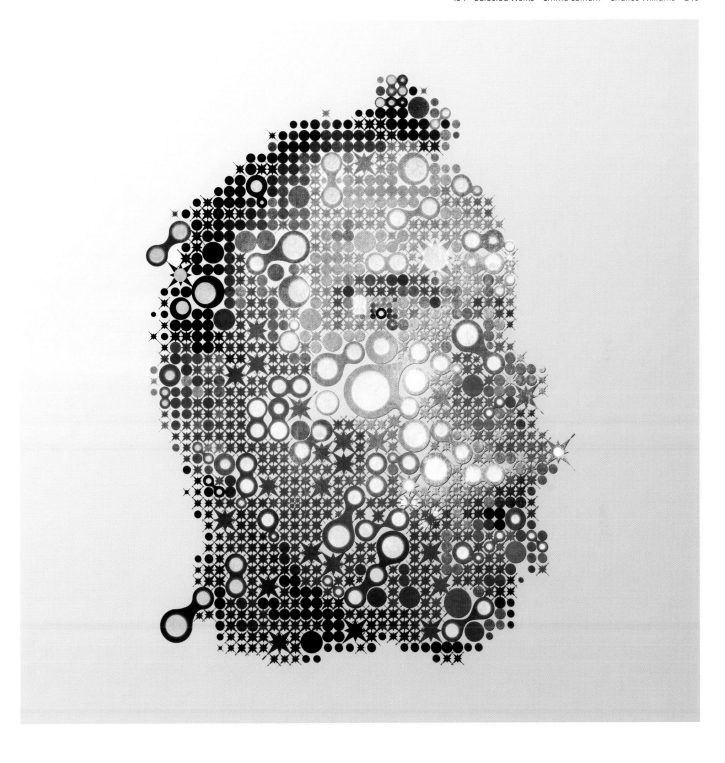

<

Emma Latham
Dogdrum
Category Self Promotion
Medium Digital and mixed media
Brief To illustrate a humorous self written
children's book following the daily antics
of a mischievous drum.

Charles Williams
Freeze
Category Self Promotion
Medium Digital and mixed media
Brief I like (amongst other things) creating
artworks from geometric patterns. I'm passionate
about illustration and typography, and have
produced work for clients including Samsung,
the BBC, Tuborg and Adidas.

Paul Wearing
Vases In Black And Brown
Category Self Promotion
Medium Digital
Brief Limited Edition Print.

Max Ellis
JG Ballard
Category Editorial
Medium Digital
Brief Create an arresting image to accompany the author JG Ballards last short story, written specially for the Guardian.
Commissioned by Roger Browning
Client The Guardian News & Media

Nicola Rowsell
Fire On The Mountain
Category Self Promotion
Medium Acrylic and digital
Brief Self initiated work for William Golding's
book 'The Lord of the Flies'.

Men To Meat (Where's The Glory?)
Category Self Promotion
Medium Ink, photocopies, gel pens, chalk,
colouring pencils
Brief A self initiated piece of work exploring and
questioning the glorification of war.

Dawn Fincham
The Plant Fairy
Category Self Promotion
Medium Digital
Brief Personal work.

Andrew Foster
Kiehl's, Restorative Dry Oil
Category Self Promotion
Medium Mixed media
Brief To capture the essence of Morocco, a journal of discovery and the ingredients of their new product.
Commissioned by Victoria Maddocks
Client Kiehl's, New York

Peter Ra
Obama, New Sheriff In Town
Category Self Promotion
Medium Digital
Brief The new president looking for peace.

Bushfires
Category Self Promotion
Medium Digital
Brief Bushfires - Black Saturday in Victoria, Australia, 2009.

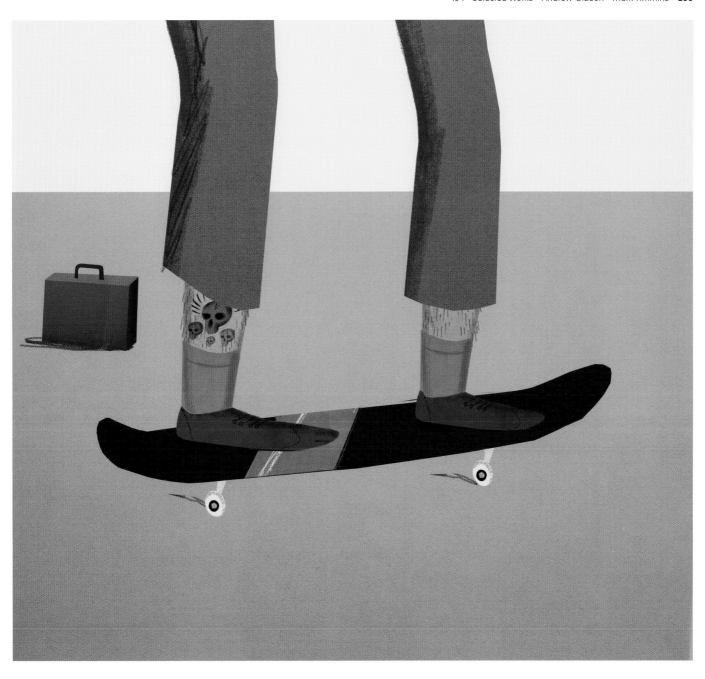

‹

Andrew Gibson
PQ
Category Self Promotion
Medium Digital and mixed media
Brief Self-promotional piece examining the
frustration and confusion in childhood dyslexia.

Mark Timmins
Thirtysomething Skaters
Category Self Promotion
Medium Digital and mixed media
Brief To illustrate an article about
thirtysomething city types reliving their
youth and returning to skateboarding.

Andy Potts
BBC Proms 2009
Category Advertising
Medium Digital and mixed media
Brief To create the main brand image to promote the BBC Proms 2009 at the Albert Hall.
Commissioned by Martin Premm
Client Premm Design
Commissioned for BBC

I Love NY, Fall
Category Advertising
Medium Digital and mixed media
Brief To create an image promoting the natural beauty of upper New York state and the sights of Manhattan.
Commissioned by Marcie Heffron
Client Saatchi & Saatchi, NYC
Commissioned for I Love New York Tourist Board

China Goes Shopping
Category Editorial
Medium Digital and mixed media
Brief Illustration about China expanding its reach overseas and buying up large companies in various sectors.
Commissioned by Christine Silver
Client Business Week

Professional Development
Category Editorial
Medium Digital and mixed media
Brief To create the cover illustration for a Design Week supplement focusing on professional development.
Commissioned by Sam Freeman
Client Design Week

Fossil Glanville
Slopes Christmas Card
Category Self Promotion
Medium Digital
Brief To design a self-promotional Christmas card to send to clients and friends.

Emma Houlston
Island of Instability
Category Editorial
Medium Ink
Brief A black and white editorial illustration for The New York Times of a cityscape of Antananarivo, Madagascar, hinting at the current social and political instability described in the adjoining article.
Commissioned by Leanne Shapton
Client The New York Times

David Bromley
Megumi's House
Category Self Promotion
Medium Lino print
Brief I wanted to create a linocut of a Japanese
theme; an image with strong blacks but bold colours.

Stuart Briers
Electricity Comes From Other Planets
Category Self Promotion
Medium Digital and mixed media
Brief Submission for a projected book on
illustrated rock music lyrics. Each image
depicting a lyric from a chosen song.

The Life Of Riley
Category Self Promotion
Medium Digital and mixed media
Brief Based on a novella about a character called
Riley who 'despite his complete lack of personality
achieved great success.'
Commissioned by Dave Garner
Client Tucson

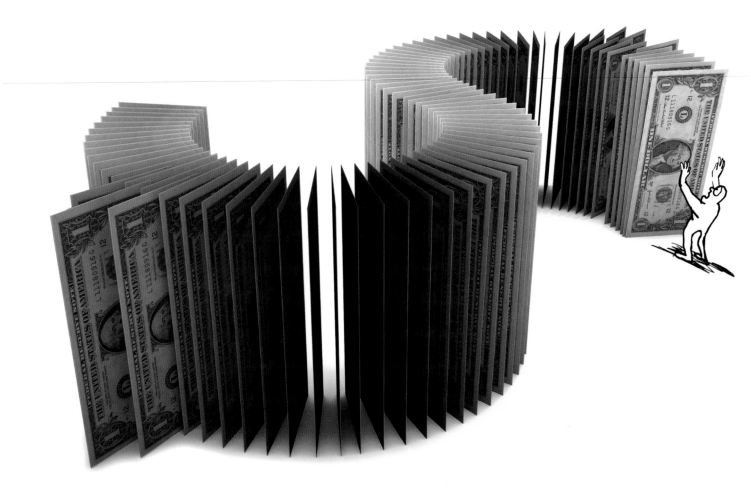

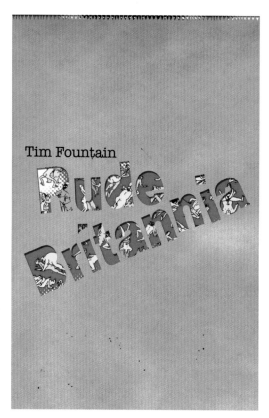

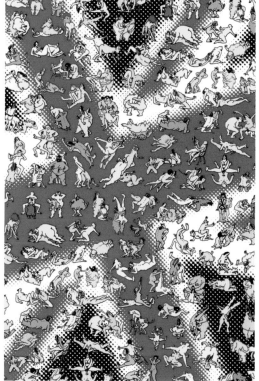

Artbombers
Dollar Dominos
Category Editorial
Medium Digital and mixed media
Brief To illustrate "Myths Of the Recession" article.
Commissioned by Leah Purcell
Client Newsweek

Rude Britania
Category Books
Medium Digital and mixed media
Brief To design the cover for Tim Fountain's
risqué Rude Britannia.
Commissioned by Steve Marking
Client Orion Books

Henning Löhlein
Like Munchhausen
Category Books
Medium Digital and mixed media
Brief The character of the book is the "problem killer", helping out where he can. Text on page reads: "A cinema hero, who can pull himself out of the biggest mud".
Commissioned by Ulla Mothes
Client Hoffmann & Campe

Honoured Banker
Category Self Promotion
Medium Digital and mixed media
Brief Money gives you status - the honoured banker.

Terry Hand
Word Disposal
Category Self Promotion
Medium Digital and mixed media
Brief The fragile nature of a love of language.

Louise Cunningham
Blackpool Donkeys
Category Design
Medium Digital and mixed media
Brief From a series of 12 designs, designed to
celebrate 'Britishness'. The brief was to create
images which had a nostalgic edge, but reflected
the Britain in which we live today.
Commissioned by Nicole Mendelsohn
Client The Almanac Gallery

Jeff Huang
Memoir
Category Self Promotion
Medium Digital and mixed media
Brief Based on a surreal relationship experience that I went through. Plenty of symbolism and meaning in this piece, but it is best left for open interpretations.

2030AD
Category Self Promotion
Medium Digital and mixed media
Brief Photo manipulation of a photo of Julia Dunin-Brzezinska. Inspired by my fascination with androids, technology and everything in between. Before and After shot could be seen at thefifthorder.net

David Hughes
Walking The Dog
Category Books
Medium Pencil
Brief A page from the graphic novel Walking
The Dog. Approaching 50 and warned by his
doctor that he's drinking too much and needs
to take more exercise the artist is given a dog
for his birthday.
Commissioned by Dan Franklin
Client Jonathan Cape
Commissioned for Walking The Dog

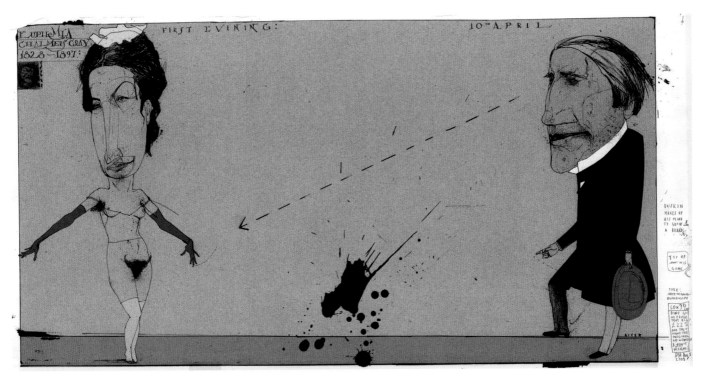

David Hughes
2009 Prediction: Stockport County Win
Promotion to The Championship?
Category Editorial
Medium Pencil and Photoshop
Brief The theme is some kind of joke/observation/
reflection on what's headed our way either next year
or further ahead. We'd like you to do something in a
single G2 page shape....
Commissioned by Paul Howlett and Richard Turley
Client The Guardian G2

Euphemism
Category Books
Medium Mixed media and Computer
Brief Art critic John Ruskin's inaugural address at the
opening of Cambridge School of Art 1858 on Sight. It
was rumoured that his marriage was unconsummated
due to a fear of pubic hair.
Commissioned by Martin Salisbury and Jim Butler
Client Anglia Ruskin University
Commissioned for Cambridge School of Art 1858-2008

Stravinsky Rite
Category Editorial
Medium Ink
Brief Portrait of composer Igor Stravinsky.
Commissioned by Christine Curry
Client The New Yorker Magazine
Commissioned for The New Yorker Magazine

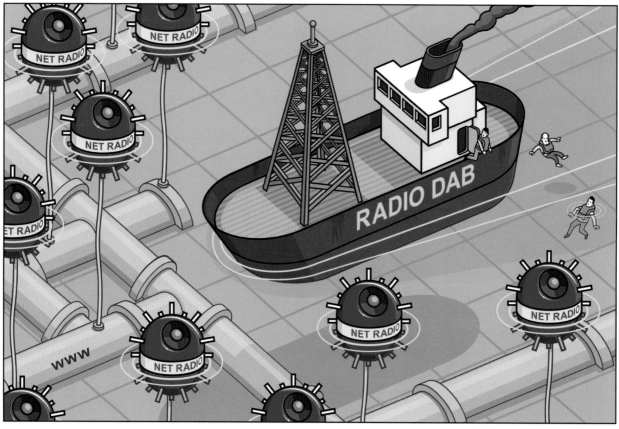

Nathan Daniels
Adobe Air Tornado
Category Editorial
Medium Digital
Brief How Adobe Air applications work
differently to normal software and their
extraordinary powers.
Commissioned by Camille Neilson
Client Dennis Publishing
Commissioned for MacUser magazine

Dab Radio Minefield
Category Editorial
Medium Digital
Brief Does internet radio spell the
end for DAB broadcasts?
Commissioned by Phill Fields
Client Haymarket
Commissioned for Stuff magazine

James Reekie
My Air Supply Was Cut Off
Category Self Promotion
Medium Digital
Brief Double page spread for the picture book/
graphic novel "Today Was Not A Good Day"
written and illustrated by James Reekie.

Laura Meredith
Nan And Moggy
Category Self Promotion
Medium Mixed media
Brief Christmas card
image printed and sent
out to mailing list.

Jay Taylor
After Life
Category Self Promotion
Medium Mixed media
Brief This is one image from a self-promotional
book I sent out called 'Throw-Away Art' and is
based on the theme of things we as human
beings throw away. This one being the after life.

Domestic Violence
Category Editorial
Medium Mixed media
Brief The brief was simply to illustrate a domestic
violence scene, but it was important to have a
woman on the phone, as if calling for help.
Commissioned by Judy Skidmore
Client EMAP
Commissioned for Health Service Journal

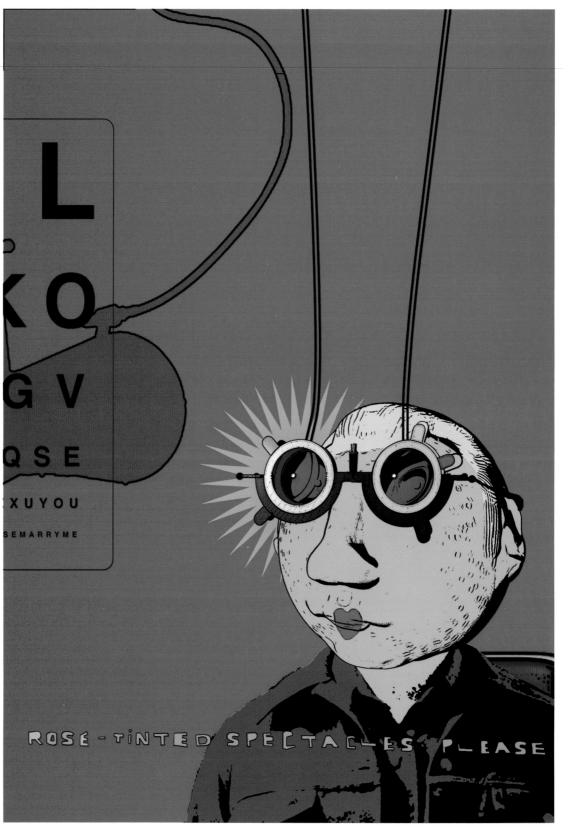

ROSE-TINTED SPECTACLES PLEASE

Mike Stones
Looking For Love
Category Self Promotion
Medium Digital
Brief To produce a series of editorial
illustrations for a promotional website.

Beautiful Creature
Category Self Promotion
Medium Digital
Brief To produce a series of editorial
illustration for a promotional website.

Paul Bateman
Ageing And Health
Category Editorial
Medium Collage
Brief Commissioned for 'Flora' Vitality
Magazine for a feature on staying healthy
in both body & mind as you get older.
Commissioned by Jenny Taylor
Client Colombus Communications
Commissioned for Vitality Magazine

Local
Category Design
Medium Collage
Brief The brief was to incorporate imagery to
reflect the courses available to students and
landmarks, into the word Local which was
used in the phrase 'Making Learning Local'
for mobile centre.
Commissioned by Al Fuller
Client Hippo Design
Commissioned for Northumberland College

Dream Destinations
Category Advertising
Medium Collage
Brief One of four images commissioned for
Expedia, advertising 'dream destinations'. This
illustration was for 'beach holidays', the others
were New York, Europe & Asia.
Commissioned by Emma Chapman
Client Meterorite
Commissioned for Expedia

Daniela Jaglenka Terrazzini
The Seeing Stick
Category Children's Books
Medium Mixed media
Brief To paint a set of pictures for a re-edition
of The Seeing Stick.
Commissioned by Frances J. Soo Ping Chow
Client Running Press Kids

John O'Leary
Motor Mouse! The Incredible Pop-up
Maze Book
Category Children's Books
Medium Ink, conté, pencil, photoshop
Brief My brief was to develop and produce text, illustrations and pop-ups for Motor Mouse!, a children's picture book adventure with 3D mazes
Commissioned by Sheri Safran
Client Tango Books
Commissioned for Tango Books

It's Magic
Category Children's Books
Medium Ink, conté, pencil, photoshop
Brief As the author/illustrator of It's Magic, my brief was to develop and produce text, illustrations and pop-ups for my own concept for this children's book, featuring the amazing Carlos Chameleon.
Commissioned by Sheri Safran
Client Tango Books
Commissioned for Tango Books

Design by Johnny Kelly www.studiodcr.ag.net
Photography by Linda Brownlee www.n3bi.a.ntian.net

Johnny Kelly
Don't Panic Poster
Category Advertising
Medium Paper
Brief The brief was "Democracy". My idea was to represent the human head as a voting system, with the brain being the government, and the lights being off.
Commissioned by Joseph Wade
Client Don't Panic

Lasse Skarbovik
Furniture
Category Advertising
Medium Digital
Brief Advertising for Santander Consumer bank in Norway: Newspaper, TV and web.
Commissioned by Kenneth Hansen
Client Lovechild

Amputate
Category Self Promotion
Medium Digital
Brief Illustration for a wall print.

Nancy Tolford
Cowboys Of The West / Vaqueros Del Oeste
Category Self Promotion
Medium Digital
Brief A personal piece inspired by the stories of a man who grew up in a family of cowboys in Mexico.

Welcome To Mexico!
Category Self Promotion
Medium Digital
Brief To create an alternative travel poster for Mexico.

White Wedding
Category Editorial
Medium Digital
Brief A new bride, who was a virgin on her wedding day, writes to say that she is developing an obsessive curiosity about her husband's previous girlfriends.
Commissioned by Martin Harrison
Client The Saturday Times

Adam Graff
The Amazing Illustrated Shed
Category Self Promotion
Medium Mixed media
Brief A culmination of 2 years MA study, this installation explores essential life themes through memories of my childhood spent in a large, wooden structure that I used as a den.

Fish Bones
Category Self Promotion
Medium Mixed media
Brief Shed installation detail referring to my school-boy interest in burying dead animals then digging them up.

Absent Father
Category Self Promotion
Medium Mixed media
Brief Shed installation detail responding to the death of my father through Asbestosis.

Pets
Category Self Promotion
Medium Mixed media
Brief Spread from a small, eight page, self-promotional booklet exploring childhood themes.

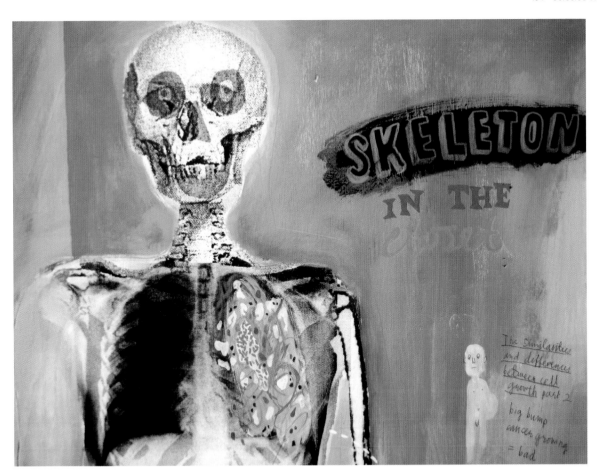

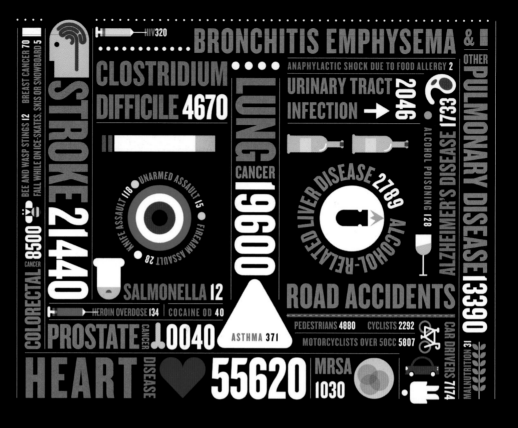

HIV 320
BRONCHITIS EMPHYSEMA & OTHER PULMONARY DISEASE 13390
BREAST CANCER 70
FALL WHILE ON ICE-SKATES, SKIS OR SNOWBOARD 5
BEE AND WASP STINGS 12
CLOSTRIDIUM DIFFICILE 4670
ANAPHYLACTIC SHOCK DUE TO FOOD ALLERGY 2
URINARY TRACT INFECTION → 2046
ALZHEIMER'S DISEASE 1733
ALCOHOL POISONING 128
STROKE 21440
LUNG CANCER 19600
UNARMED ASSAULT 15
KNIFE ASSAULT 118
FIREARM ASSAULT 28
ALCOHOL-RELATED LIVER DISEASE 2789
COLORECTAL CANCER 8500
SALMONELLA 12
HEROIN OVERDOSE 134   COCAINE OD 40
ROAD ACCIDENTS
PROSTATE CANCER 10040
ASTHMA 371
PEDESTRIANS 4880   CYCLISTS 2292
MOTORCYCLISTS OVER 50CC 5807
CAR DRIVERS 7174
MALNUTRITION 31
HEART DISEASE 55620
MRSA 1030

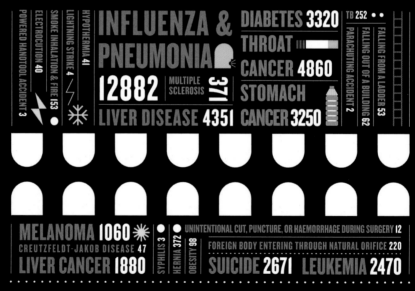

POWERED HANDTOOL ACCIDENT 3
ELECTROCUTION 40
SMOKE INHALATION & FIRE 153
LIGHTNING STRIKE 4
HYPOTHERMIA 41
INFLUENZA & PNEUMONIA
DIABETES 3320
TB 252
FALLING FROM A LADDER 53
FALLING OUT OF A BUILDING 62
PARACHUTING ACCIDENT 2
THROAT CANCER 4860
12882
MULTIPLE SCLEROSIS 371
STOMACH CANCER 3250
LIVER DISEASE 4351

MELANOMA 1060
CREUTZFELDT-JAKOB DISEASE 47
SYPHILIS 3
HERNIA 372
OBESITY 98
UNINTENTIONAL CUT, PUNCTURE, OR HAEMORRHAGE DURING SURGERY 12
FOREIGN BODY ENTERING THROUGH NATURAL ORIFICE 220
LIVER CANCER 1880
SUICIDE 2671   LEUKEMIA 2470

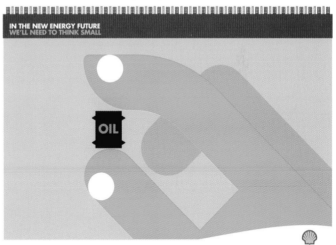

Peter Grundy
Skull
Category Editorial
Medium Digital
Brief DPS for Mens Health magazine, listing UK deaths in amounts from various ailments from heart disease (55620) to falling off a ladder (53).
Commissioned by kerem shefik
Client Mens Health magazine

Shell New Energy Future
Category Advertising
Medium Digital
Brief Create a visual language to communicate complex messages about Shell's new responsible Energy future.
Commissioned by Julia Parry
Client JWT
Commissioned for Shell International

The growing cycle

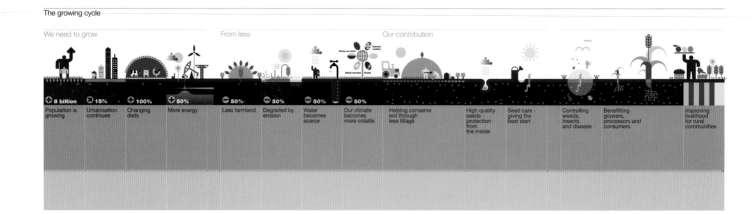

We need to grow | From less | Our contribution

⊕ 8 billion	⊘ 15%	⊕ 100%	⊕ 50%	⊖ 50%	⊖ 50%	⊖ 50%	⊖ 50%					

Population is growing · Urbanisation continues · Changing diets · More energy · Less farmland · Degraded by erosion · Water becomes scarce · Our climate becomes more volatile · Helping conserve soil through less tillage · High quality seeds - protection from the inside · Seed care - giving the best start · Controlling weeds, insects and disease · Benefitting growers, processors and consumers · Improving livelihood for rural communities

Kiss your partner somewhere they've never been kissed before.

SOUTH WEST TRAINS

Discover that there is life outside London.

SOUTH WEST TRAINS

'Say oops up side your head.'

SOUTH WEST TRAINS

We are pleased to annouce the new Doris Ledbetter timetable.

SOUTH WEST TRAINS

Introducing Oliver Dunkley's new timetable.

SOUTH WEST TRAINS

Save your money for shoes that don't quite fit and you'll never wear.

SOUTH WEST TRAINS

Don't fear machines.. Except the Terminator.

SOUTH WEST TRAINS

Things you can command from your ticket machine.

SOUTH WEST TRAINS

Peter Grundy
The Growing Process
Category Design
Medium Digital
Brief A 2 DPS diagram to explain the agriculture growing process for the Syngenta annual report.
Commissioned by Clive Newman
Client Radley Yeldar
Commissioned for Syngenta

South West Trains Poster Campaign
Category Advertising
Medium Digital
Brief Create a set of amusing iconographic characters to illustrate snappy headings for tube and stations.
Commissioned by Rupert Simmonds Gooding
Client M&C Saachi
Commissioned for South West Trains

Proudly introducing the new Charles Pym timetable.

SOUTH WEST TRAINS

2 nights for I in Hampshire, remember to leave enough food for Henry.

SOUTH WEST TRAINS

For sale 2 for I tickets at the Motor Museum, No previous owner.

SOUTH WEST TRAINS

What's the rush? There are trains every 3-4 minutes.

SOUTH WEST TRAINS

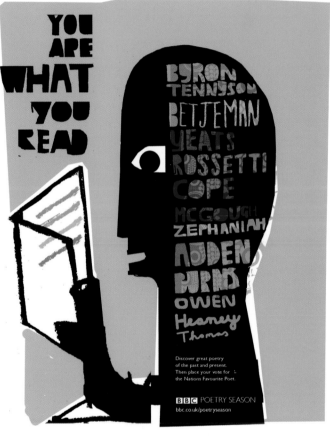

Chris Haughton
He Wishes For The Cloths Of Heaven
Category Advertising
Medium Digital
Brief Illustration for WB Yeat's poem 'He wishes
for the Cloths of Heaven'. One in a series of ten
postcards to promote BBC Poetry season.
Commissioned by Martin Premm
Client Premm Design

BBC Poetry Season Poster
Category Advertising
Medium Digital
Brief Poster to promote BBC Poetry Season.
Commissioned by Martin Premm
Client Premm Design

Stephen Simpson
SweetTalk34
Category Self Promotion
Medium Digital and mixed media
Brief Poster created for Sweettalk 34, the
illustration night. Used to promote the event
and as giveaways on the night.

M.H. Jeeves
Lipstick Ladies
Category Self Promotion
Medium Ink and collage
Brief Image produced juxtaposing magazine &
drawn images of women (for my own amusement).

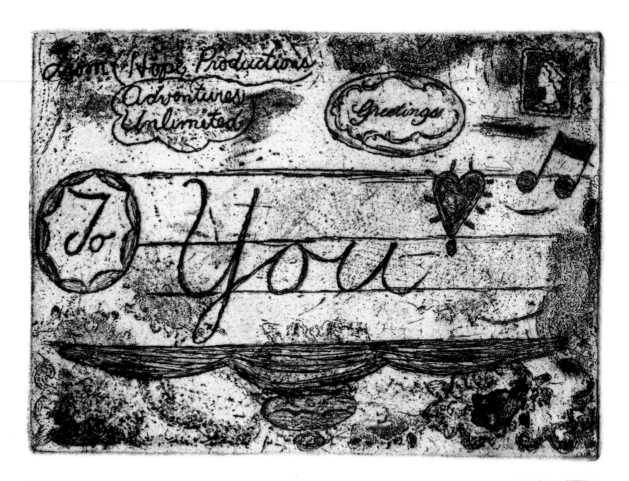

Carolyn Gowdy
To You
The Real Thing
Category Self Promotion
Medium Mixed media
Brief Two of a series of
printworks produced for
ongoing 'Life is an Adventure,
Life is a Gift ...' project.

The State We're In
Category Design
Medium Mixed media
Brief Set based on my
interpretation of civil liberties
campaigner, Brian Haw's
peace camp. He has camped
in London's Parliament
Square 24/7 for eight years.
Client Zeitgeist Theatre
Commissioned for
Edinburgh Fringe Festival

Works by full-time students, including those graduated in 2009.

Janet Woolley has been working as an Illustrator in the UK and USA for over 30 years, with clients that include: Rolling Stone Magazine, Time Magazine, The Washington Post, The Guardian, MTV, Penguin Books and the BBC, Elle Magazine, Newsweek.

She was an Associative Lecturer at Central Saint Martins for 16 years both on the BA and MA Illustration courses, and was made a Visiting Professor in 1996.

She is now the Subject Leader for MA Illustration at Camberwell College of Art, a Patron of the AOI and a member of the Society of Illustrators in New York, awards include: 'Benson and Hedges Gold Award for Illustration', 'D&AD Award for Press Advertising', International Advertising Festival, Lions '95, Cannes - Press and Poster - Bronze Award, Society of Illustrators, USA - Silver Medal (Advertising), USA 'Art directors Club Award', New York Society of Illustration - Gold Medal and 'The Association of Illustrators' Images 31 Gold Award for promotional work'.

She has recently completed a series of murals for 'The Royal Institute of Science' London.

What do I say to a group of illustration students embarking on a new career in the creative arts, in this atmosphere of economic gloom and despondency? 2009 had the potential to be one of the most depressing years ever. Not so, as it turned out! A positive and exciting year lay ahead.

The students were committed, motivated, and tenacious in their approach to personal growth, creative development and professional progress. I would go as far as to say that there was almost a feeling of renaissance in the air in the field of illustration and at art colleges. Never has the subject been so diverse and the students so innovative; initiating their own exhibitions, online activity, events, promotions, producing work so playful, experimental, and yet at times so seriously committed.

More than ever before, students are looking deeply into what they actually want from their life and what is important to them. As these works show, they remain devoted to the subject creating work that is inventive and fresh. Again and again, visiting practitioners to the college have commented to me about the enthusiasm and passion of students, and the inspiration they have felt when working with them.

Hearty congratulations to the winners of 'New Talent'. A selection of thoughtful and exciting pieces; the ambition and social integrity of work by Chun-Sheng Tsou, the playful magic of Masako Kubo, the humour and charm of Alex Bitskoff and the charismatic experimentation and design of Linsey Spinks and Rhys Bevan-Jones.

This selection of work provides a welcome mood of optimism; willingness to takes risks, professionalism, and commitment to the subject.

Emerging illustrators need all of the encouragement and support we can give them. They are in the early phase of a career that demands commitment and fortitude alongside their talent and creativity. This is a time when they will be considering the basic concerns such as where they will work, whether they need to work with a group in a shared environment, or alone, and how to market their illustration work.

They will be reflecting upon issues such as where their personal boundaries lie, both morally and financially, and considering what they believe in, and how and where their work will sit within the field of communications. This can be an extremely exciting time, but not without serious challenges and anxieties.

In these challenging times, the need for self-belief and commitment, and the ability to develop and create your own work is clear. Many established illustrators have also taken the opportunity in these quieter times to experiment and develop their portfolios.

Venturing into new areas, taking risks, reflecting upon the past and looking to the future, are things we all need to consider, established practitioners and newcomers alike. My opinion is that the newcomers are far more equipped and ready to brave these elements.

A really good illustration can connect with the public consciousness, can influence thoughts, engage the heart or shock us to our core. It can make us laugh, inspire us and appeal to our conscience.

Students are constantly asked to research through their work and learn from the past, discover their personal strengths and reflect upon their weaknesses, experiment, take risks and contextualise their work. They are asked to develop a personal visual language that they can take in to the world of commissions, to be realistic and aware of professional issues, know their audience, and be able to negotiate and understand the pressures that the commissioners are faced with concerning creative freedom and budget restrictions. Name me a more challenging brief if you can!

Conversations with the emerging illustrators in 2009 have, as always, included topics such as the balance between personal work and commissions and how one can enhance the other. We often discuss illustration fees, briefings, and the best way to promote and market their work, and what environment they should work in. I have on many occasions talked over how important it is that Illustrators retain a professional attitude to their work, in areas such as

timekeeping and the importance of listening to the client.

So imagine my disappointment on receiving regularly, as I do, calls from students asking whether they should take on commissions with no fee, or a more recent emerging trend of free pitching, all common, but none the less bad practice.

Examples: An ex-student is asked to send their folder to a publisher, told they almost certainly have a cover, but asked to work one up with no fee so that they, the client can decide for sure! Then adding that they can't yet give them an estimate of the final fee even if they are indeed chosen. Or, a new illustrator is asked to develop and storyboard a book with no fee offered.

In what other profession would this occur? Could we take a product from a shop or indeed a painting from a gallery, not pay, go back a month later and decide how much or if indeed we wish to pay at all? We all understand that companies are under pressure to cut expenditure and have very little finance to invest in illustration, but this is an appeal to a small number of commissioners and editors: Please take time to view and engage with these talented emerging illustrators and if you commission them, treat them as the professionals that they are. Pay them even if it is a initial down payment to show some regard for the profession. They are the future of illustration and need the encouragement of the industry.

These new illustrators as you can clearly see from this 'New Talent' selection, are keeping the flame of illustration burning brightly. They have invested their time and talent in the Art of Illustration.

Britain has a long history of producing some of the most innovative and inspiring illustrators. There is a real feeling of excitement and a buzz in the industry at present, and the future is in the good hands of these newcomers and the commitment of established illustrators. But the responsibility for the future potential of this art rests to some extent in the hands of the commissioners and editors working now.

i34 • New Talent • Essay
Professor Janet Woolley • Illustrator and Educator

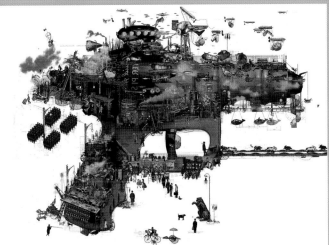

THE SLOW DEATH OF HANDWRITTING.

Kathryn Spreadbury
A strong idea based piece that retains
a sense of energy and experimentation.
Echoes of Ben Shahn.

Joanne Young
I would love to see this Illustration work
in a children's book. There are glimpses
of traditional British book Illustration, the
darkness of 'Where The Wild Things Are'
and an eccentricity and imagination that
warms the heart.

Rick Bellin
An example of brave experimentation
and imagination. An emotional image with
integrity and verve.

Kristien Harris
Energetic, simple and nearly a perfect idea.

Alex Bitskoff
Humour and warmth, with that touch of the
inner child and madness that certain
children's books need.

Chun-Sheng Tsou
This piece has craftsmanship, drawing skills,
a strong idea and good design. This illustration
shows an intelligent approach to a subject that
in other hands could have resulted in an overly
grim or clichéd image. But this is an engaging
and thought- provoking piece of Illustration.

Sponsored by The Coningsby Gallery

Kathryn Spreadbury • Urban Jungle

Kathryn Spreadbury was inspired by visiting Canary Wharf in London and doing observational drawings, which sparked her to write a narrative 'Urban Jungle' that then became the back bone of creating her images. This particular image is part of the series.

Kathryn likes to use a wide variety of media in her work including, charcoal and ink, in which she used to create this dark, dirty atmosphere.

Kathryn graduated from UCA Maidstone in 2009 and is currently living and working in Maidstone, Kent.

College UCA Maidstone
Medium Charcoal and ink
Brief An excerpt from a project about the life of a business man. The workers are insignificant little minions while a great dark, overpowering shadow looms above. Inspired by observations made in London.
Course BA (Hons) Illustration
Head of Department Neil Breeden
Course Leader Astrid Chesney

i34 • New Talent Refresh! Award • Silver

Sponsored by The Coningsby Gallery
James Portch • Electromagnetic Pulse

James Portch is a 23 year old illustrator based in the Midlands and London. James enjoys creating images that have depth, character and something to make you smile. He is also interested in how simple imagery with a strong concept can communicate complex subjects.

College Sheffield Hallam University
Medium Screenprint
Brief Based on an article found within the New Scientist magazine: The article was about electromagnetic pulses being used as a form of terrorism to take down planes.
Course BA Graphic Design
Head of Department Frazer Hudson
Course Leader Lee Ford

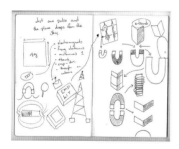

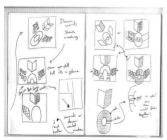

i34 • New Talent Refresh! Award • Bronze

Sponsored by The Coningsby Gallery

Shuning Qian • Animal's Secret

Shuning Qian was born in China in 1985. In 2007 she graduated from Visual Communication Department of China Academy of Art. Currently, she lives in Loughborough, and studies as a MA Graphic student in Sheffield Hallam University, working on her final project about an independent magazine.

College Sheffield Hallam University
Medium Ink
Brief Four pictures in a series, my work describes stories between diverse animals, full of metaphors, a space for viewer to think and imagine.
Course MA Graphic Desgin
Head of Department Steve Bort
Course Leader Lee Ford

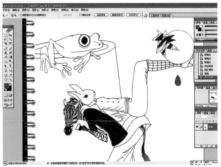

Each entry is marked by the jury
according to how well the work fulfils
the brief, originality, and technical
ability. Only the highest scoring images
are invited to feature in the annual.

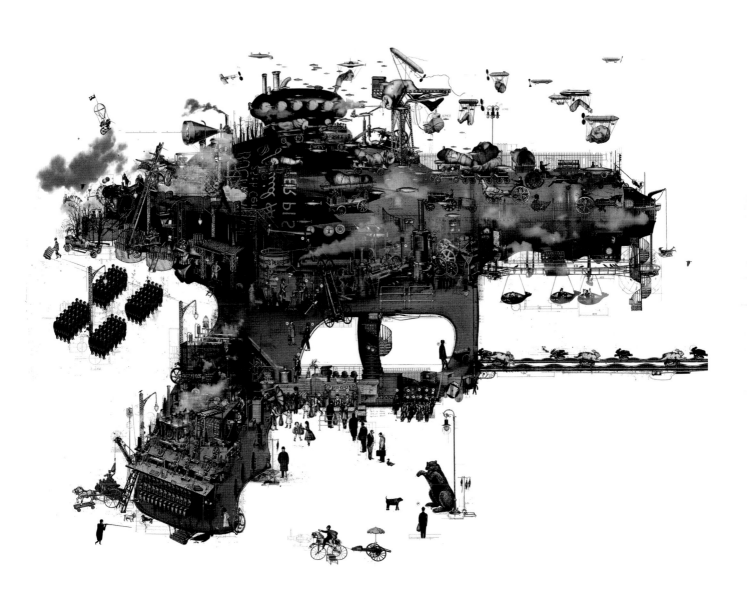

Chun-Sheng Tsou
The Gift That Keeps On Giving
College Royal College of Art
Medium Digital and mixed media
Brief I grew up in a factory, was a primary school
teacher, and spent 2 years in military service. I say:
Toy guns are related to education and violence.
Course MA Communication Art & Design
Course Leader Catherine Anyango

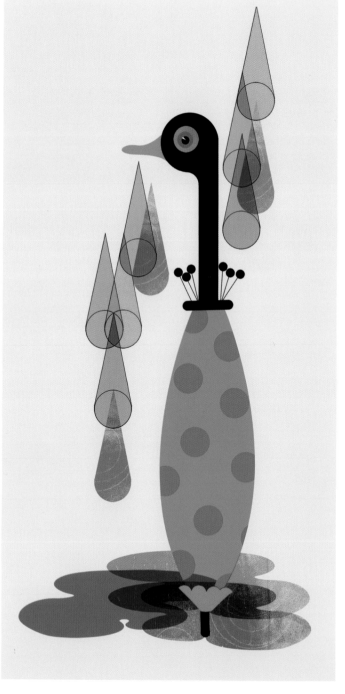

Rose Lloyd
Beware
College Stockport
Medium Digital and mixed media
Brief Major project - Holidays.
To avoid an upset stomach when
travelling abroad, do not eat unwashed
fruit and vegetables.
Course BA (Hons) Design & Visual Arts
Course Leader Ian Murray

Brolly
College Stockport
Medium Digital and mixed media
Brief Major project - Holidays.
When visiting Britain always have
a brolly handy.
Course BA (Hons) Design & Visual Arts
Course Leader Ian Murray

Masako Kubo
It Is Not Only Fine Feathers That Make Fine Birds
College University College Falmouth
Medium Digital and mixed media
Brief Image for a book of illustrated quotes and sayings.
Course BA Illustration
Course Leader Alan Male

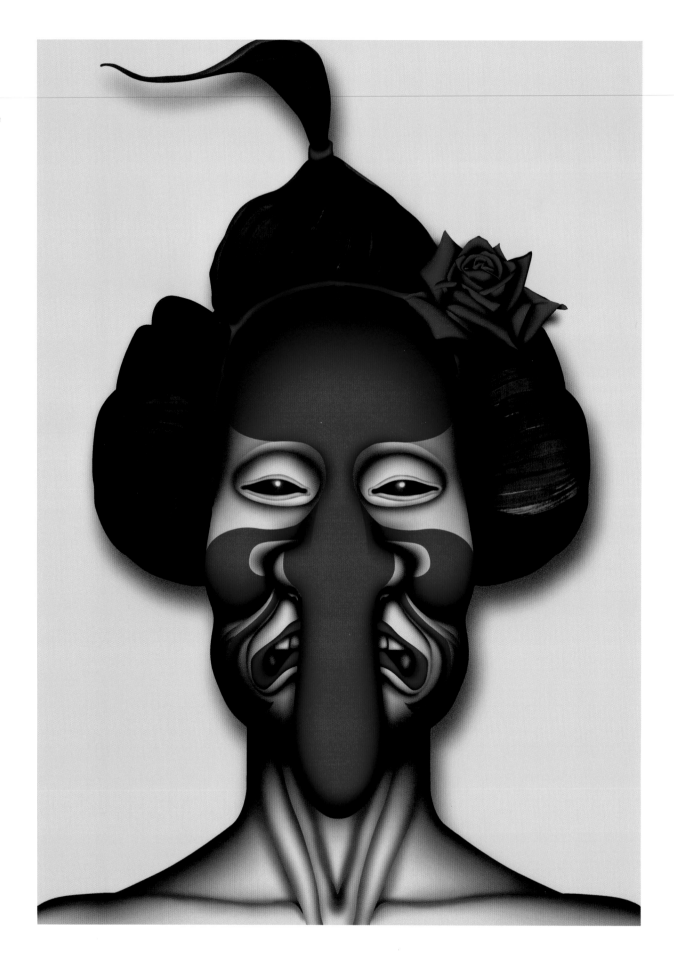

Okapi

Dan Stafford
Funeral Parade Of Roses
College Loughborough University
Medium Digital and mixed media
Brief Explore Japan's conflicting cultures
to produce a DVD cover image for Toshio
Matsumoto's post-modern film making
masterpiece, Funeral Parade of Roses.
Course BA (Hons) Illustration
Course Leader Andrew Selby

Tom Coombs
Okapi
College University Of Hertfordshire
Medium Mixed media
Brief Level 3 Illustration Brief; Create a piece
of work that serves to promote you as an image
maker, problem solver and creative thinker.
The work can be made in any appropriate
medium or format.
Course BA (Hons) Graphic Design & Illustration
Course Leader Cathie Felstead

Lindsey Spinks
Helen The Hypochondriac
College Kingston University
Medium Mixed media
Brief Self initiated project about
Hypochondria. The aim to explore
the individuals behind the illness.
To create a light hearted piece that
could also offer support to a sufferer.
Course BA (Hons) Illustration
Course Leader Geoff Grandfield

THE SLOW DEATH OF HANDWRITING.

" Strangers arrived at the court "

Kristien Harris
The Emperors New Clothes
College University College Falmouth
Medium Acrylic and ink
Brief Shed new light on the Hans Christian
Andersen fairy tale, for a modern audience.
The content is to embrace the themes of
deception, vanity and self representation.
Course BA (Hons) Illustration
Course Leader Alan Male

The Slow Death Of Handwriting
College University College Falmouth
Medium Ink
Brief To produce an illustration for the BBC
website article "The Slow Death of Handwriting".
In order to illuminate the current displacement
of analog writing by computer technology.
Course BA (Hons) Illustration
Course Leader Alan Male

Cheism
Night Time Police
College University Of Westminster
Medium Acrylic
Brief Exploring night time in London for an editorial on crime and representing the familiar in a different light.
Course BA (Hons) Illustration
Course Leader Elizabeth Grob

Stefano Terranova
Sunset On Dump Beach - Democratic Dictatorship Of Phestonia
College London College Of Communication
Medium Digital and mixed media
Brief To produce postcards and stamps from the imaginary island of Phestonia. Self promotion.
Course ABC Certficate in Illustration
Course Leader Karl Foster

Tom Hunt
Conversation Injection System
College Edinburgh College of Art
Medium Pencil
Brief I was asked to produce an image dealing with conversations in pubs. Beer became the lubricant of choice for the gears of the chatter-machine.
Course Illustration MFA
Course Leader Jonathan Gibbs

Jeansoo Chang
Circus: Falling
College Maryland Institute College of Art
Medium Watercolour
Brief This sequential illustration is from the series of my commencement exhibition. I designed the animal character based on the theme circus; targeting baby & toddler market. The original size is 5"x25".
Course Senior Thesis I
Course Leader Rebecca Bradley

Aidan Meighan
Expansion
College University Of Western England
Medium Drawn in pen
Brief Home is in the countryside but I live in
Bristol during term time, this blur of identities
has made me unintentionally obsessed in the
transition between the country and the city.
Course Illustration
Course Leader Gary Embury

Fiona Dunphy
Winter
College Liverpool School Of Art, John Moores
Medium Digital and mixed media
Brief The brief was to create a series of covers
for a collection of seasonal short stories.
Course BA (Hons) Graphic Arts (Illustration)
Course Leader Michael O'Shaughnessy

Big Meat Pizza
College Liverpool School Of Art, John Moores
Medium Digital and mixed media
Brief To create an illustration for an article
about a man that wants his girlfriend to watch
pornography with him.
Course BA (Hons) Graphic Arts (Illustration)
Course Leader Michael O'Shaughnessy

Ollie Stone
The Beast 2
College Southampton Solent University
Medium Ink, Acrylic Paint, Pen, Pencil,
Watercolour, Crayon, and Photoshop
Brief A re-vamped work, that was the
final piece for my Illustration degree in
2009. The building, painted and drawn,
had the imagery layered into it, and
was displayed as an 8 foot tall work.
Course BA (Hons) Illustration
Course Leader Peter Lloyd

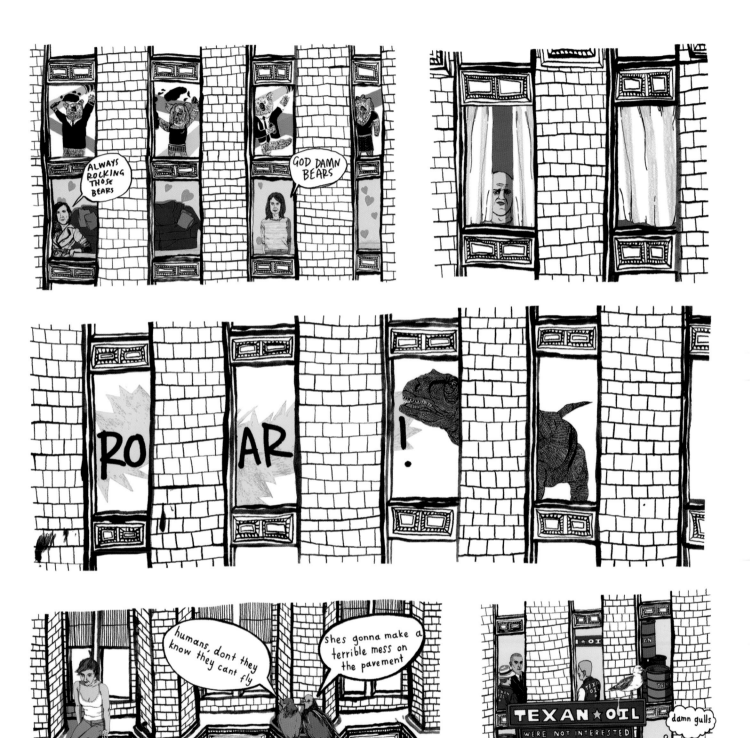

Paul Williams
Head Down
College Stafford University
Medium Digital and mixed media
Brief To create a range of merchandise designs
for an online store for the band Nine Inch Nails.
Live Assignment.
Course Creative Arts for Employment: Illustration
Course Leader Neil Wood

Matthew Long
Fabulous Babylon
College Southampton Solent University
Medium Ink, pen and fineliner
Brief Open brief. The work depicts a
gambling-addicted metropolis, home
to a vast array of creatures and casinos,
with some buildings playfully resembling
chance-related paraphernalia.
Course BA (Hons) Illustration
Course Leader Peter Lloyd

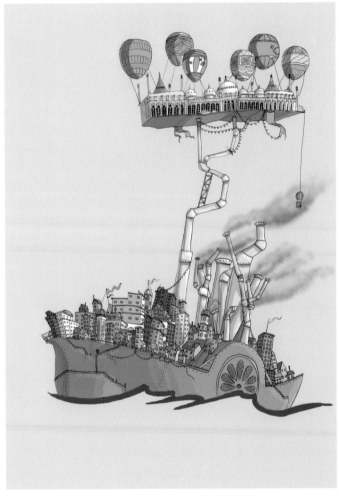

Kellie Black
British Summertime (Inspired by Dana Bethea)
College University of Westminster
Medium Acrylic
Brief This piece was created as part of a project entitled 'Life on Earth'. I interpreted the brief in a literal manner by looking at perspectives from the ground upwards, which served to also demonstrate the changes in climate.
Course BA (Hons) Illustration
Course Leader Elizabeth Grob

Kirsty Mordaunt
Airhaven
College University Of Lincoln
Medium Pencil and digital
Brief Produce a series of images from Philip Reeve's Mortal Engines Quartet.
Course BA (Hons) Illustration
Course Leader Howard Pemberton

Brighton
College University Of Lincoln
Medium Pencil and digital
Brief Produce a series of images from Philip Reeve's Mortal Engines Quartet.
Course BA (Hons) Illustration
Course Leader Howard Pemberton

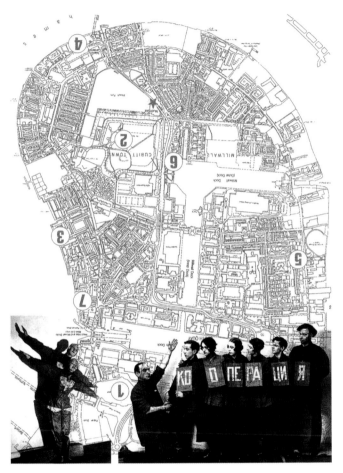

Patrick Stewardson
Def of an Artist
College Norwich University College of Art
Medium Acrylic and ink
Brief Second panel of a story about the death
of an artist and his obsession with air vents.
Course BA (Hons) Graphic Design (Illustration)
Course Leader Rob Mason

Jenny Vaughan
Aleatory
College Norwich University College Of The Arts
Medium Screenprint
Brief To produce a concept book based on
the word 'aleatory'. All images were created
using a random generating system, resulting in
everything in the book being brought together
entirely by chance.
Course BA (Hons) Graphic Design: Illustration
Course Leader Robert Mason / Glyn Brewerton

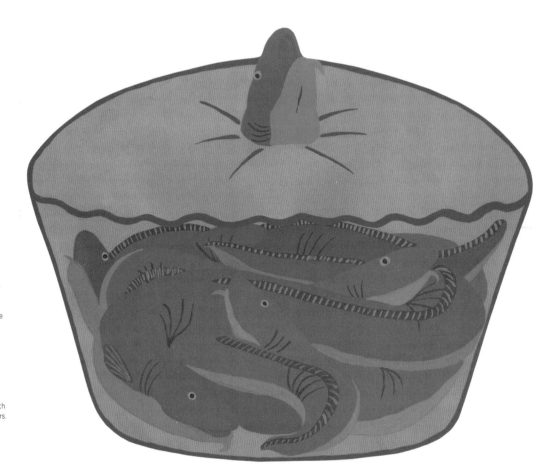

Emma Cowley
Yorkshire Christmas Pie
College University Of Westminster
Medium Gouache
Brief Great British Pies: Standing pies such
as this were popular in Victorian times.
They would be made in Yorkshire and
transported to London for Christmas, where
they were often given as gifts.
Course BA (Hons) Illustration
Course Leader Elizabeth Grob

Eel Pie
College University Of Westminster
Medium Gouache
Brief Great British Pies: Illustrations of
traditional British pies, the contents of which
may seem strange to contemporary viewers.
Eel Pies have long been a working class
food synonymous with London.
Course BA (Hons) Illustration
Course Leader Elizabeth Grob

Donya Todd
Catboy
College University of Plymouth
Medium Acrylic and ink
Brief To illustrate personal narrative, Catland,
about a girl and a boy who change into a cat.
Course BA (Hons) Illustration
Course Leader Ashley Potter

Philip Harris
M Is For Market
College University of Plymouth
Medium Dip pen and Ink
Brief Use a simple format to show off personal
imaginative approach.
Course BA (Hons) Illustration
Course Leader Ashley Potter

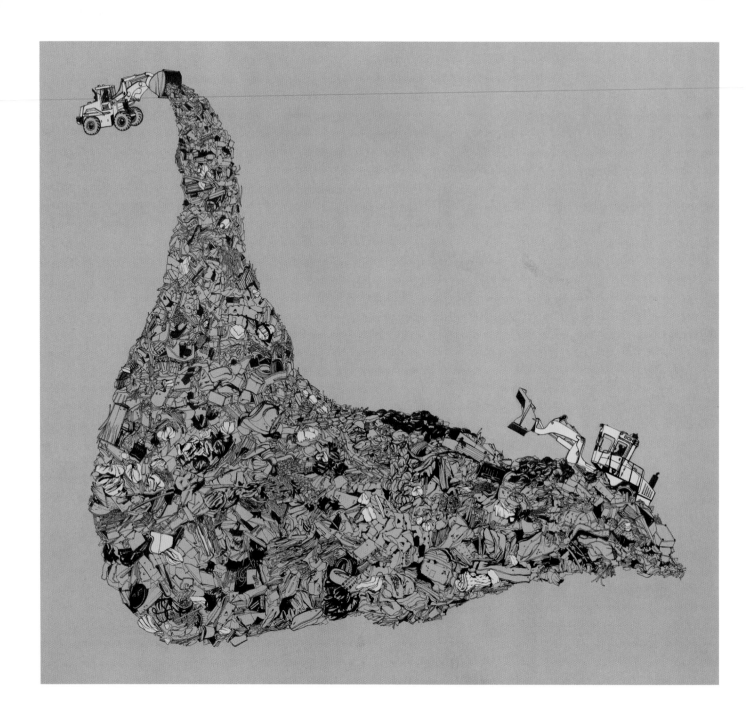

Ben Williams
The Landfillers
College Norwich University College of the Arts
Medium Acrylic and fineliner pen
Brief Based on observation, this piece acts as a
reminder of the consequences of modern living
and to make that extra effort to recycle.
Course BA (Hons) Graphic Design (Illustration)
Course Leader Robert Mason

Darren Cranmer
Awfulising
College Arts University College At Bournemouth
Medium Digital and mixed media
Brief This image intends to represent anxiety related
illness and the growing, spiralling and polluting
momentum that anxious thought generates.
Course BA (Hons) Illustration
Course Leader Matt Johnson

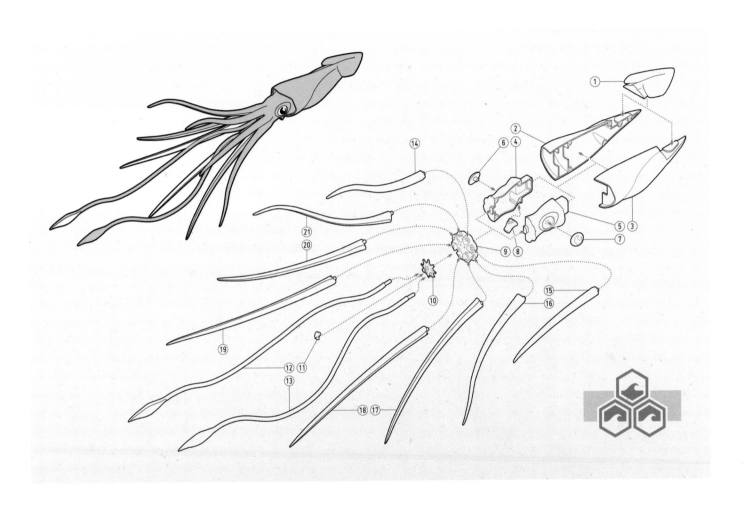

Tommy Webb
Golden Bear
College Central Saint Martins
Medium Etching
Brief Inspired by a protest from my past where
a supermarket was built on a green field site.
Course MA Illustration
Course Leader Andrew Foster

Robert Goldsmith
Self-assembly Cephalopod
College University Of Lincoln
Medium Digital
Brief This was a self initiated project, exploring
the limitations of isometric projection through
unconventional subject matter.
Course BA (Hons) Illustration
Course Leader Howard Pemberton

Anna Violet
Mousey And The Scary Climate Change Monster
College Stockport College
Medium Mixed media
Brief A3 double page spread inside children's book.
Mousey gets advice from different creatures (bee,
snail, fox and chameleon) on how to tackle the
climate change monster.
Course BA (Hons) Design & Visual Arts (Illustration)
Course Leader Ian Murray

Joanne Young
The Forgotten Birds Of The British Isles
College NUCA
Medium Ink and watercolour
Brief To create discovered pages from 'The
Forgotten Birds of the British Isles', a take on
original bird manuals where hybrid characters
have been created and set in various places
throughout Britain.
Course BA (Hons.) Graphic Design (Illustration)
Course Leader Glyn Brewerton

94. CROSS SECTION OF BIRDS FROM THE CORNISH COUNTRYSIDE.

1. A female Dusky Camellia, *Identification:* Large: 10 feet. 2. Marsh Polypodium (male), *Voice:* A deep, repeated *yurrr-yarrr-yarrr,* lacking the terminal *aw* of the Barred Polypodium. 3. Marsh Polypodium (female), main characteristic is its extendable neck. 4. Black-throated Primula malacoide. 5. Unknown. 6.

Threaded Woolenwake, *main identification:* hanging beak. 7. Cornish Kingianum (mother) watching over nest made with her back feathers. 8. A family of Woven Hymenocallis, main characteristic is their aggressive nature.

UNLEASHED

Northern School of Design

<

Alex Barratt
Unleashed
College University Of Central Lancashire
Medium Digital and mixed media
Brief Design a Poster for university's
degree illustration exhibition.
Course BA (Hons) Illustration
Course Leader Steve Wilkin

Anna Suwalowska
Dinner
College University Of The Arts London
(Camberwell College Of Arts)
Medium Mixed media
Brief The illustration presents a man
transformed gradually into a monster by
his greedy consumption.
Course Illustration
Course Leader Luise Vormittag

Rob Gill
We Are What You Eat - Anti Litter Campaign
College University Of Central Lancashire
Medium Digital and mixed media
Brief Illustrate the issue of litter and leftover food.
Making people aware of the animals and pests
that live off our waste.
Course BA (Hons) Illustration
Course Leader Steve Wilkin

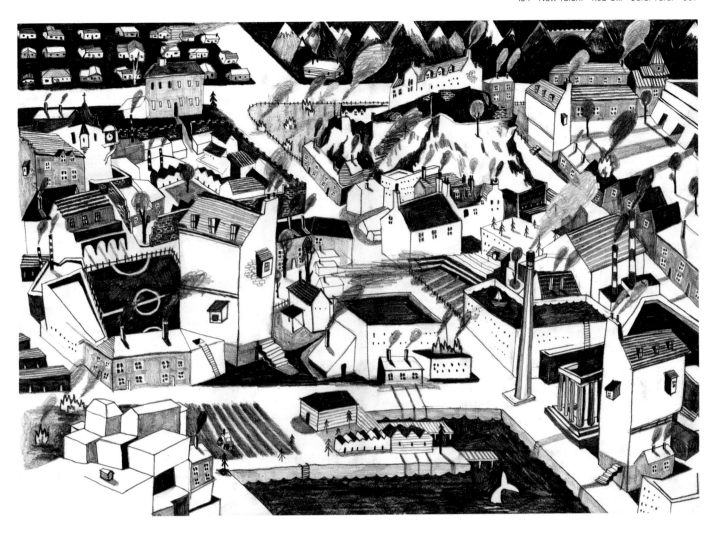

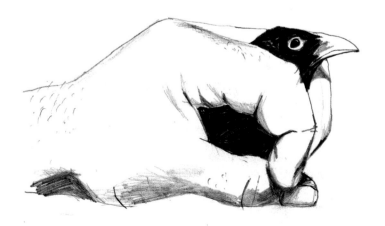

Sarai Vardi
Metropolis
College Kingston University
Medium Pencil
Brief To create a personal cityscape loosely
based on my home town, Edinburgh.
Course BA (Hons) Illustration and Animation
Course Leader Geoff Grandfield

Caught
College Kingston University
Medium Pencil
Brief To illustrate artwork for a post rock
record sleeve.
Course BA (Hons) Illustration and Animation
Course Leader Geoff Grandfield

Rick Bellin
The Fall Of Babylon
College Southampton Solent University
Medium Digital and mixed media
Brief From the path of the obelisk, the fall
of Babylon.
Course BA (Hons) Illustration
Course Leader Edward Chaney

Jerusalem
College Southampton Solent University
Medium Digital and mixed media
Brief I created a book called the Path of the
Obelisk, its an illustrated historical graphic novel
recording a lost history, the image derives from
one of the pages: Jerusalem.
Course BA (Hons) Illustration
Course Leader Edward Chaney

Sara Mulvanny
The Big Bad Wolf Handbook
College Kingston University
Medium Digital and mixed media
Brief This is from a children's book I made called
'The Big Bad Wolf Handbook' in which the Three
Little Pigs have scribbled over the pages to
ridicule and confuse any wolf reading the guide.
Course Illustration and Animation BA (Hons)
Course Leader Geoff Grandfield

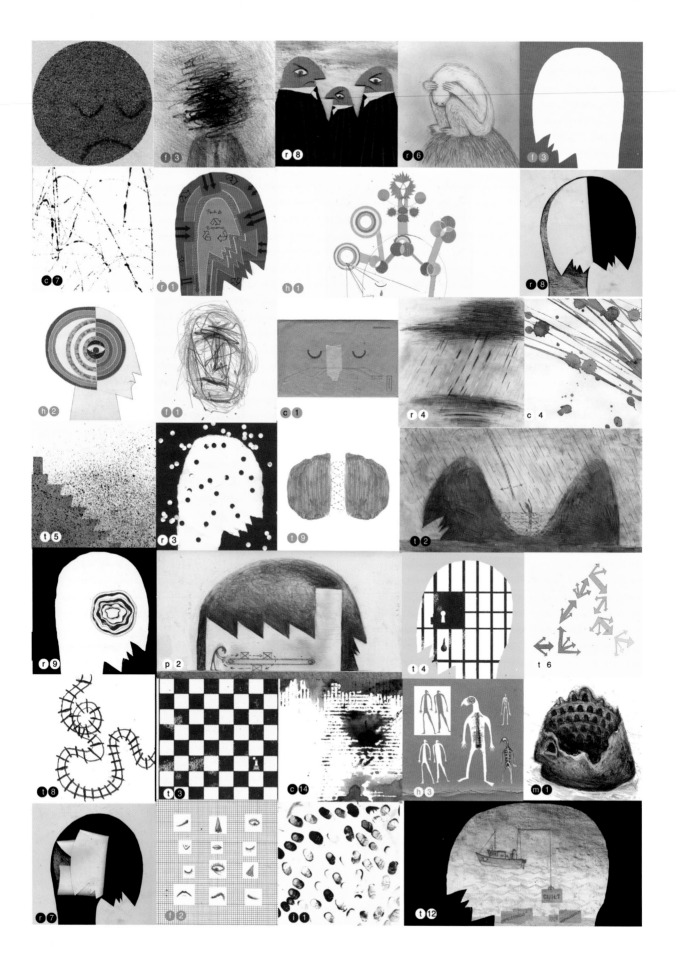

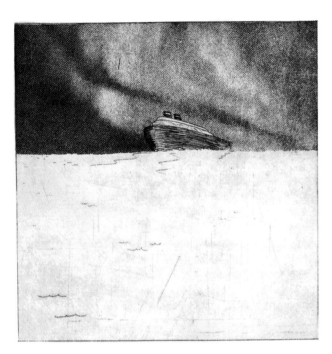

Rhys Bevan Jones
Depression
College Kingston University
Medium Digital and mixed media
Brief I have worked in mental health and am interested in the expression of mental states. I illustrated how friends and family 'saw' depression, and am exploring the application in therapy and education.
Course BA (Hons) Illustration and Animation
Course Leader Geoff Grandfield

Denise Hobson
Return
College Coventry University
Medium Etching
Brief Self directed brief to create a visual novel based on the memories and photographs of my parents' emigration to Canada and their subsequent return in the 1950s.
Course Fine Art & Illustration BA Hons
Course Leader Glyn Brewerton/ Francis Lowe

Junk male

from planet 'PewBerty'.

Louise Todd
Junk Male
College Dumfries and Galloway College
Medium Digital
Brief Create an eye catching image to use on a
t-shirt for an online t-shirt design competition.
Course HND Visual Communication
Course Leader Penny Humphreys

Catherine Sweetman
My Sister Is An Alien
College University Of Derby
Medium ink and water colour
Brief Independent study module. A children's
picture book exploring puberty from a younger
siblings viewpoint.
Course BA (Hons) Visual Communication (illustration)
Course Leader Tracy Tomlinson

Peter's Jungle
College University Of Derby
Medium Acrylic and ink
Brief A children's picture book exploring loneliness.
The length of Peter's tangles causes children to stare
but looking up close they see more to this boy and
join in the fun with laughter and joy.
Course BA (Hons) Visual Communication (illustration)
Course Leader Tracy Tomlinson

>

Jake Richardson
Poodle Skirt
College Lincoln College (Newark)
Medium Digital and mixed media
Brief '1950s mini book of quotes'. A book and zine
project based around the 20th Century decades.
Course Graphic Design National Diploma
Course Leader Helen Mather

Monroe
College Lincoln College (Newark)
Medium Digital and mixed media
Brief Mini book project based on the 20th Century
decades (focus 1950's).
Course Graphic Design National Diploma
Course Leader Helen Mather

Alex Bitskoff
The Tree
College Camberwell College Of Arts
Medium Digital and mixed media
Brief Bad guy tells stories, but only Tree
knows the truth.
Course MA Visual Arts
Course Leader Janet Woolley

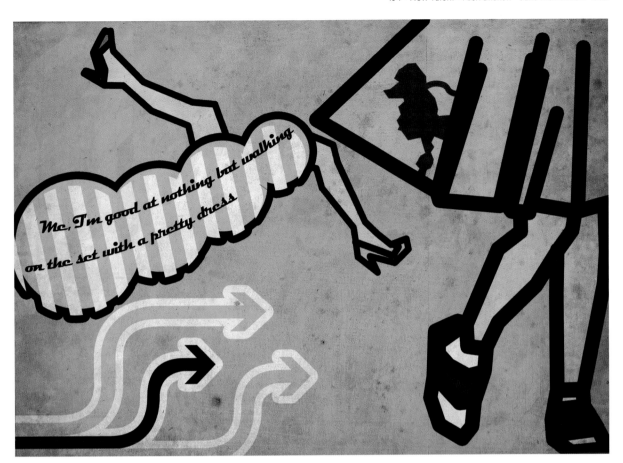

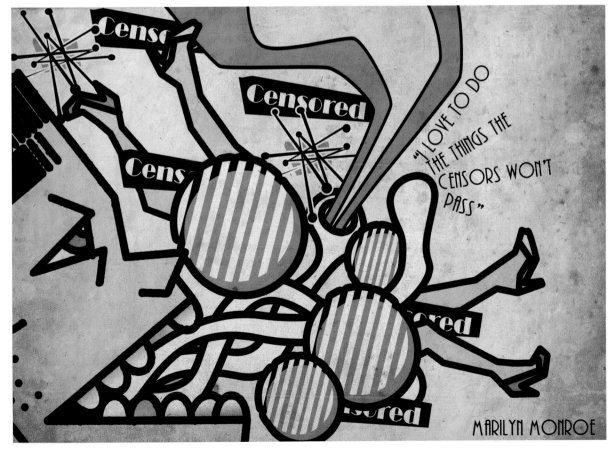

David Thelwell
And Sang To A Small Guitar
College Southampton Solent University
Medium Etching with watercolour
Brief University project/self promotion.
Course BA (Hons) Illustration
Course Leader Peter Lloyd

They Danced By The Light Of The Moon
College Southampton Solent University
Medium Etching and watercolour
Brief Illustration for university project/self promotion.
Course BA (Hons) Illustration
Course Leader Peter Lloyd

>
Jonathan Penn
'…In Brogues'
College Royal College of Art
Medium Pencil on paper
Brief Fashion Illustration/Animation Character
Course MA Fashion Design Womenswear
Course Leader Julie Verhoeven

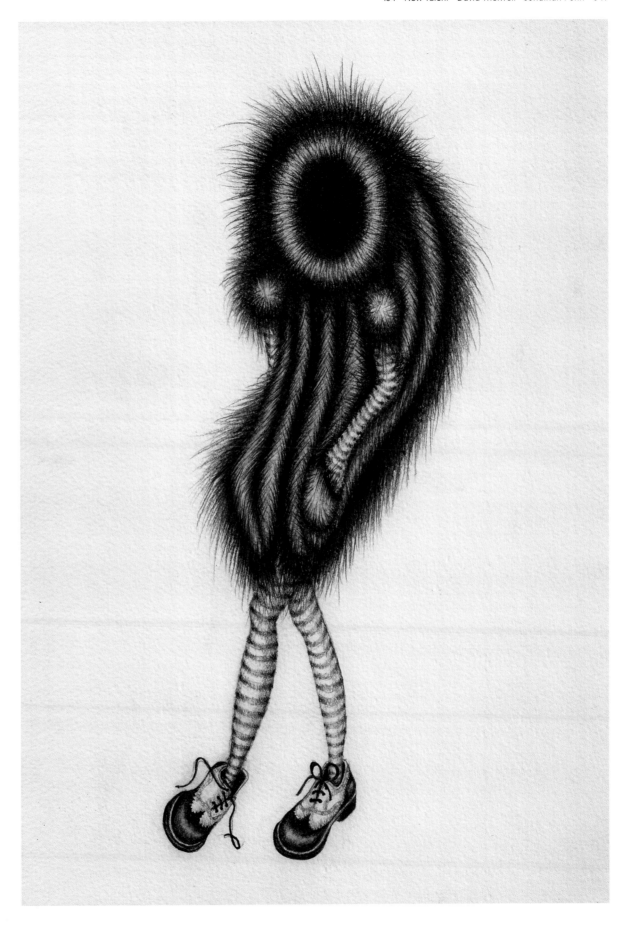

Ami Shin
Janet Klein
College Kingston University
Medium Digital
Brief This is a character which implies
Janet Klein, the traditional ukulele jazz
singer in California.
Course Illustration and Animation
Course Leader Geoff Grandfield

Janet Klein And Her Parlor Boys
College Kingston University
Medium Digital
Brief I created a character by making
her pulling-up-skirt pose harmonious
with British afternoon tea.
Course Illustration and Animation
Course Leader Geoff Grandfield

Darpan Sunwar
Funky Lady
College University Of Hertfordshire
Medium Screen print and digital
Brief Character designed for my upcoming
interactive education children book.
Course BA (Hons) Graphic Design and Illustration
Course Leader Jim Stoten

>

Indre Brazdzionyte
Kew Gardens
College Middlesex University
Medium Etching
Brief One of a series of etchings based
on the environment of Kew Gardens, for a
project on the theme of Hidden London.
Course BA (Hons) Illustration
Course Leader Nancy Slonims

The Mushroom Pickers
College Middlesex University
Medium Etching
Brief One of a set of etchings bound into
an illustrated edition of Indre's own story,
The Mushroom Pickers.
Course BA (Hons) Illustration
Course Leader Nancy Slonims

Annie Driscoll
Boy Number 3
College Middlesex University
Medium Mixed media, dip pen and ink
Brief An illustration from a book developed to
support the animated film in the same style.
Course BA (Hons) Illustration
Course Leader Nancy Slonims

Julie Mackey
Best In Show
College Middlesex University
Medium Screenprint
Brief To design a proposal for a poster for
the Middlesex University Graphic Design,
Illustration & Photography degree show.
Course BA (Hons) Illustration
Course Leader Nancy Slonims

Emma Codner
Rebecca
College Middlesex University
Medium Screenprint
Brief One of a series of screenprinted
A1 posters promoting classic black and
white films at the NFT.
Course BA (Hons) Illustration
Course Leader Nancy Slonims

Town
College Middlesex University
Medium Etching
Brief One of a set of etchings with aquatint,
illustrating Under Milk Wood by Dylan Thomas.
Course BA (Hons) Illustration
Course Leader Nancy Slonims

The AOI would like to thank:
All members of the jury for applying
their expertise to the difficult task of
selecting the best of all the entries now
published in this book. As always, to
Sabine Reimer, Images Co-ordinator, for
her efficiency and cheerful dedication
during the production of Images 34.
Special thanks go to Simon Sharville
for his creative involvement during the
design process.

Frazer Hudson, whose image
"Loudhailer" was used for the
promotion of the call for entry for
Images 34.

Images 34 could not have been
organised without the help of our
dedicated casual staff and volunteers
and we are very grateful for their
invaluable assistance.

Last but not least, we are grateful for
the support of the many organisations
and individuals who contribute to the
success of the Images exhibition and
annual by submitting their work for
others to judge.

The AOI Board and staff

i34 • About the AOI

The Association of Illustrators was established in 1973 to advance and protect illustrators' rights. It is a non-profit making trade association dedicated to its members' professional interests and the promotion of contemporary illustration. As the only body to represent illustrators and campaign for their rights in the UK, the AOI has successfully increased the standing of illustration as a profession and improved the commercial and ethical conditions of employment for illustrators. On behalf of its members and with their continued support, the AOI can achieve goals that it would be difficult or impossible for creators to attempt alone.

A voice for illustration
The AOI provides a voice for professional illustrators and by weight of numbers and expertise is able to work at enforcing the rights of freelance illustrators at every stage of their careers. AOI liaises with national and international organisations, agents and illustrators over industry problems and campaigns against unfair contracts and terms of trade.

Campaigning
The AOI was responsible for establishing the right for illustrators to retain ownership of their artwork and helped to establish the secondary rights arm of the Designers and Artists Copyright Society (DACS), the UK visual arts collecting society. In addition, it lobbies parliament for better legislation for illustrators through the British Copyright Council (BCC) and the Creators Rights Alliance (CRA). The AOI is also a founder member of the European Illustrators Forum (EIF), a network of 20 member associations in Europe established to exchange information, co-ordinate exhibitions and conferences and create a stronger force for illustrators within Europe.

Pro-Action: Illustration Campaign and Liaison Group
The Pro-Action committee was established by the AOI and the Society of Artists Agents to deal with the problems facing illustrators in today's market place. The aims of the group

are to tackle fee erosion, increasingly detrimental contract terms from clients and issues that may arise between illustrators and their representatives. These factors have increasingly become a negative force affecting creators of visual material working in the commercial communications arena over the last 25 years.

For further information please visit www.pro-action.org.uk

Information and Support Services
AOI continues to improve services to its members, and ensures they are kept up to date with relevant industry information. Members of the AOI not only sustain campaigning and networking to improve working conditions for all, they benefit personally from AOI services.

Members stay informed with our wide range of events and seminars. 'Varoom' magazine and the twice-monthly 'UPmail' email newsletter keep members up to date with events, practice and developments in the industry. Members receive up to 50% off our topical range of events and forums, themes ranging from children's books, to self-promotion, business planning and up-to-the-minute industry debates.

Resources to help illustrators succeed
Members receive large discounts on essential publications, including the Images annual, The Illustrator's Guide to Law and Business Practice and our range of targeted directory listings of illustration commissioners. Members of the AOI receive discounts in art shops around the country.

Resources to help commissioners succeed
The AOI's Guide to Commissioning Illustration saves time and money by guiding commissioners safely through the pitfalls of the commissioning process. Commissioners receive Images, the definitive jury-selected source book in the UK, free of charge. Our online portfolios at AOIportfolios. com give commissioners looking for the perfect artist for their projects access to more than 15000 classified images and the creator's contact details in a click.

Essential professional and business advice
Members have access to a free dedicated hotline for legal, ethical and pricing advice, discounted consultations with our pool of industry specialists including business advisors, a chartered accountant and a portfolio consultant.

Promotion
Members can receive substantial discounts on the AOI's online portfolios at AOIportfolios.com and our Images competition and exhibition, showcasing the best of British contemporary illustration. The annual is despatched to over 4000 prominent commissioners of illustration in the UK and overseas. All information on Images can be found at AOIimages.com

Inspiration
Talks with leading illustrators, industry debates and discounted entry to competitions and exhibitions. Members receive a free subscription to Varoom magazine - a sumptuous celebration of illustration and its role within culture and society. Featuring interviews with leading illustrators and image-makers as well as in-depth articles on different aspects and themes of contemporary illustration. Its stimulating line-up of interviews, profiles, history and polemic make 'Varoom' essential reading for everyone interested in visual communication. See more at varoom-mag.com

Contact
To request further information or a membership application form please telephone +44 (0)20 7613 4328 or email info@theaoi.com

Website
Visit the AOI's website at theAOI.com for details of the Association's activities, details of forthcoming events and online tickets, listings and reviews, the AOI's history, and to purchase publications or view online portfolios.

Association of illustrators

Publications

The illustrator's Guide to Law and Business Practice
This comprehensive manual covers all aspects of the law likely to affect illustrators. It contains recommended terms and conditions, advice on calculating fees, how to write a licence agreement and be protected against exploitative practices.

Interspersed with contemporary illustrations, the handbook was written by Simon Stern, a renowned expert on illustration and the law, and is the result of many years of research. It has been approved by intellectual property experts, law firm Finers Stephens Innocent.

Client directories
AOI produce three essential Directories. The Publishing Directory lists circa 170, and the Editorial Directory more than 280 illustration clients with full contact details; the Advertising Directory holds details of about 150 advertising agencies who commission illustration – providing an invaluable source of information for all practitioners. Each directory includes notes of what kind of illustration is published by the client and we update and add contact details to each list every year. CD ROMs are also supplied with addresses and pre-formatted labels for printing.

Varoom – illustration, culture, society
Varoom is devoted to exploring the world of illustration and image-making. The magazine looks at practitioners from around the world who are making significant contributions to the constantly evolving art of illustration, on both a commercial and culturally significant level. Varoom provides writers, commentators and illustrators with a platform from which to take a critical yet accessible look at trends and developments in the illustrated image.

Published three times a year. 88 pages, available on subscription and in specialist bookshops in the UK and worldwide, free to members.

The Varoom website has information on current and back issues, and features web-only content, reviews and articles.
varoom-mag.com

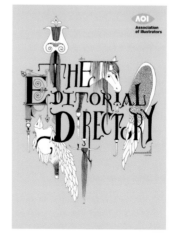

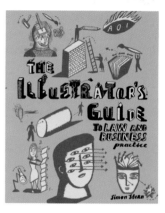

Information

Report on illustration fees and standards of pricing

This informative report was revised in April 2007 and can be found in the members section of the AOI website. It contains information from an online survey, AOI data collated over many years and invaluable contributions from agents, art buyers and selected working professionals.

Properly researched costing and pricing structures is a central plank in maintaining business viability, and illustrators should consider the true cost of their services when determining rates. AOI believes this report builds awareness of the importance of carefully considered pricing for both illustrators and commissioners.

UPmail email newsletter

UPmail, published twice monthly, brings you the latest industry news, AOI events information, campaigns, initiatives and listings of relevant exhibitions and publications.

To subscribe, visit the News section on the AOI website.

theAOI.com - illustration resources for commissioners and practitioners

Visit the website for details on AOI membership and the Association's activities, including UPmail e-newsletter, details of forthcoming events and campaigns, the AOI's history, news and reviews, and to purchase publications and tickets. The Members Only section contains exclusive articles and reviews and the AOI Pricing Survey.

To order publications online go to theAOI.com
To subscribe to Varoom go to varoom-mag.com

For further information please contact the Association of Illustrators on +44 (0)20 7613 4328 or email info@theaoi.com.

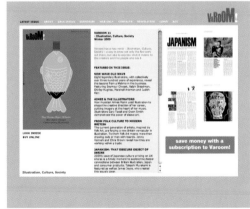